Psychology for Daily Living:

Simple Guidance in Human Relations for Parents, Teachers, and Others

E. Rae Harcum

Nelson-Hall nh Chicago

Library of Congress Cataloging in Publication Data

Harcum, Eugene Rae, 1927-
Psychology for daily living.

Bibliography: p:
Includes index.
1. Psychology. 2. Interpersonal relations.
I. Title.
BF121.H225 158 79-1048
ISBN 0-88229-384-2 (cloth)
ISEN 0-88229-686-5 (paper)

For information address Nelson-Hall Inc., Publishers, 111 North Canal Street, Chicago, Illinois 60606.

Manufactured in the United States of America

10 9 8 7 6 5 4 3 2 1

Table of Contents

To Sally and Payten,
with a father's pride and a guide's humility

Preface

Psychology for Daily Living is written primarily for persons with little or no background of study in psychology. It is a primer, a first step, giving the most basic and important principles of psychology. Its purpose is to encourage the application of general psychological principles to problems of daily living, using familiar situations as examples.

The book differs from standard introductory textbooks in four important ways: coverage, practicality, terminology, and documentation.

The present book does not try to cover every aspect of psychology in detail. The typical introductory textbook presents an encyclopedia of facts using technical graphs and formulae. The reader is therefore likely to despair of knowing what is most practical.

Although this book deals with the basic causes of all human acts, good and bad, normal and abnormal, it concentrates on the normal acts which the average person would perform. It thus avoids the danger of jumping too quickly into the study of seriously abnormal acts, which are less familiar to the layman, and which require a much greater level of understanding, skill, and familiarity with the relevant psychological principles.

This book promotes practical applications to problems of daily living by describing how the psychologist goes about understanding human behavior, rather than by listing facts and rules. The usual introductory book, unfortunately, does not maintain a focus on what the average reader wants most: help with common social and personal problems. In fact, my first reason for writing this book was to provide a textbook for a short course in psychology for adults who were training to become church school teachers. No standard introductory textbook could meet their needs; they did not need, for example, the usual descriptions of the physical structure of the eyeball, statistical methods, or the history of psychology.

Because I spend most of my time as a teacher and parent, the applications which come most readily to my mind concern college students and youth. Nevertheless, the principles are basically the same, whether the guide is a teacher, manager, supervisor, military officer, psychotherapist, or some other person in a similar relationship to another.

Because of its concern with practical applications, this book must necessarily discuss some topics, such as ethics and morality, which are not a part of psychological science. The setting of goals is necessary for effective use of psychological principles, because we cannot use a tool effectively when we do not know our purpose for using it. But the principles which produce behavior cannot, to be sure, tell us which behaviors are the desirable ones.

Psychology for Daily Living discusses the psychology of familiar situations in greatly simplified terms. I use common words as often as possible, because the technical words are not necessary for this book. Unfortunately, scientists often write in ways which impress rather than inform. For example, a part of a complicated piece of apparatus was designated in a scientific magazine as a "diagnostic port," although, as best I could determine, the indicated part would more commonly be called a "peephole."

This book is written in the style I use for talks to lay groups, such as organizations of parents, teachers, businessmen, or citizens for community action. These persons do not need to be exposed to all of the technical terms and complications of "scientific" psychology. Knowledge that the technical term "pilomotor response" means "goose pimples," or that "agoraphobia" means "fear of open places," does not provide much practical help.

Simple definitions for some words are given at the end of the book. To compose the list, I consulted glossaries in standard textbooks on introductory psychology, as well as several standard dictionaries of English words, and also a *Comprehensive Dictionary of Psychological and Psychoanalytical Terms* by English and English (1958). For students who are planning further study of psychology, I have also given an equivalent technical term for the common word when one was sufficiently close.

Almost all of the evidence in this book is provided by reference to the reader's own experiences rather than by reference to the psychological literature. The research literature is summarized in typical introductory textbooks which are easily available. Where it was helpful to mention specific works, the author's name and the year of publication are given to aid the reader in finding the reference at the end of the book.

In addition to the four major differences mentioned above between this and standard texts, this book has several other unique qualities. One of these is that it strives to overcome the faulty idea many people have that a book like this must be *either* "scientific" *or* "relevant to life"—but not both. As a teacher of psychology for twenty-two years, and an active church member for thirty-nine years, I have developed an approach to psychology that satisfies me as being accurate, practical, and moral. I trust that what I have developed will be useful to the beginning student. While my approach is generally in agreement with that of many others, it probably does not coincide in details with the views of anyone else.

Individual preferences for particular theoretical positions will therefore not pose a problem for those who use the book. The approach upon which I have based my work is called information-processing, to refer to the tendency of a person to take in information from his environment and to interpret or process it in terms of his own experience and personality. This theoretical approach is very similar to that of Dollard and Miller (1950) which employs the concepts of drive, cue, response, and reward. It also exhibits a similarity to the three-part division of the personality proposed by Sigmund Freud (1943) into id, ego, and superego. Therefore, supplementary materials can be integrated from either the biological-experimental approach to psychology or from the personality-social-adjustment point of view, with equal convenience.

The intended audience for the book is broad, because everyone should know and use the basic principles of psychology. This especially includes parents who are eager to understand their children in a changing world, and also the youth who are trying to adjust to the unclear and often conflicting demands of modern society, who anticipate the day when they themselves will have adult responsibilities.

Study of this book can aid in keeping persons on the right track toward mental health and effective human relations. The book guides the interested layman by showing him how to recognize some danger signals of psychological disturbances that indicate a particular behavioral problem may be serious enough to require professional help. The need for caution, sound judgment, and restraint in this connection is strongly stressed many times throughout the book, however. The old saying, "a little knowledge is a dangerous thing," is true for psychology. But because everyone already has a little knowledge of psychology, I am adding more knowledge in order to reduce the danger.

Study of *Psychology for Daily Living* should also improve the quality of personal life. Increased understanding of the causes of another person's acts produces new understanding about the causes of our own acts, because the same principles of behavior affect everyone. This understanding also improves our ability to get along with others harmoniously. The book should therefore be well suited for orientation programs to college life; I have used it to my satisfaction for this purpose.

This book can serve as part of a formal educational program, for example as a supplemental or core textbook for the first psychology course in high school or college. Because the emphasis is clearly on applications to daily life, the most obvious uses are in beginning courses in applied psychology or in the psychology of personal adjustment. Therefore, this book can be used as a starting point for a high school or college course, with supplementary material, such as books of readings, discussion exercises, or laboratory manuals, added according to the preference of the instructor. The college student could, for example, go on to a standard introductory text in the same semester, having read *Psychology for Daily Living* to give him an overview of one general approach to solving psychological problems. The present book is, in fact, designed to be a foundation, not a substitute, for more detailed material.

Some school systems have developed modular schedules, or "minicourses," for relatively small fractions of the school year, in which a very brief book such as this would be appropriate. *Psychology for Daily Living* can also fill a need in some continuing education courses or brief training programs for scout leaders, camp counsellors, student nurses, ward attendants, and similar workers with children and adults, as well as church school leaders. I have used it to my satisfaction in such a manner. Schoolteachers can find the book useful as a guide in developing successful learning programs, while maintaining classroom discipline; supervisors in the factory can be helped to foster increased production while still maintaining harmony among the workers; and so forth.

Not all of the many persons who have assisted in the preparation of *Psychology for Daily Living* can be named individually. The typing of initial drafts was accomplished with patient diligence by Natalie Gillette Stason. The illustrations are also largely due to the able efforts of Ms. Stason, to whom I owe an additional debt for her many helpful comments and criticisms. Special gratitude is given to the students who have used a draft of this book in my freshman seminar on the application of psychological principles to human problems, and in several continuing-education classes. Their comments and discussions have been very helpful.

Other persons, both laymen and clergy as well as professional psychologists, have constructively criticized substantial portions of the manuscript. Among this group, special thanks are given to James Brown, Peter Derks, Herbert Friedman, C. P. Minnick, and Nancy Piland. The book is greatly improved because of their conscientious assistance.

To my children, Sally and Payten, I owe gratitude for providing me with interesting examples and valuable experiences, and for their gracious good humor in permitting me to refer to them. Finally, the daily involvement of my wife, Phoebe, made the effort possible.

1. The Need for Psychology

One day as I was preparing a talk for a PTA meeting on emotional problems of teenagers, on impulse I asked my college-student assistant what in her opinion caused such problems. She quickly answered, "parents and teachers." Probably, a parent would have mentioned teenagers and teachers, and the teacher would have charged parents and teenagers. Whomever we blame for the problems, all of us have important people with whom we must live. Often our biggest daily problems are in learning how to get along with other people. In fact, our survival, both as individuals and as nations, depends upon it. Although destruction of our planet by pollution seems possible, quicker destruction by superweapons is also probable if we do not learn to control our anger at one another and to build harmonious interpersonal and international relations.

Our emotional health also is bound up in our relations with other people. Obviously, the more we come into contact with a person, and the closer that contact, the more important our problems with him become.

There are two parts to the problem of living with people. The first is that, in the future, few of us will have as much privacy as we might like. The population explosion forces people closer and closer together. It is becoming more difficult just to turn our backs and walk away from persons who irritate us, or whom we may annoy, albeit unintentionally. We turn away from one person and frequently find ourselves facing an even stiffer challenge to our ability to work with other people.

The second part of the people problem is that just coping with life situations is getting to be more complicated. There is more of almost everything connected with people and the things they use in trying to make life more comfortable. This increase in people and things means, of course, that we simply have more of them to contend with or adjust to.

These new things also may bring about new relationships among the peoples and things. For example, modern rapid transportation causes not only exposure to more people but also to people from less familiar cultural backgrounds, who prefer, say, soccer balls to baseballs or rice to potatoes. Therefore, our old attitudes and ways of adjusting to the problems of daily living often are not appropriate to the changed circumstances of life; assumptions about the ways things are may not correspond to present reality. For example, the increased urbanization of our population means that the average citizen probably cares more for automobiles and clothes than for land and the family homestead. Each new invention may force us to learn responses that were not needed before, like coping with machines for changing folding money, computers for automatic billing, self-service gasoline pumps, European road signs, and metric measurement.

The learning of new responses and attitudes is often more of a problem to older persons, because the new ideas may conflict drastically with old habits. For example, in response to student pressures and new concepts of civil liberties, college administrations have dropped many traditional social rules for students. Someone has said that today it is easier for a college student to keep a member of the opposite sex in his room than to keep a canary.

The increasing changes in our society require that some of the additional people in our lives take unfamiliar roles. Such people must be responded to differently; new adjustments are required. Some people we control, and others control us, and some we just have to learn to live with in peace.

To deal happily and effectively with other people, we must learn why human beings act the way they do—ourselves as well as others. This is the goal of psychology, the science of behavior. Psychologists investigate why man acts the way he does, and attempt to use the new knowledge to improve his behavior. Even psychologists as specialists in dealing with people lament, however, that they do not know enough about the causes for specific human acts. It is almost impossible to understand as much as we need to know about the causes of behavior.

The basic task for all fields of applied psychology is to get one person to agree to do what is best for him and for the rest of society. Good communication between persons is necessary for this. A schoolteacher once said that she never had a behavior problem once she got the attention of the child. She meant that it was first necessary to establish a receptive and cooperative attitude in the child toward that which she was trying to accomplish. Persons in authority usually understand that they must convey to their subordinates whatever information is necessary for them to do their jobs properly, but not enough of them recognize the need for willing acceptance of this information. Thus, the primary task of the guide—teacher, parent, employer, friend—is to get the other person to work willingly for the approved goals.

To be effectively helped, the person must first learn how to bring himself under sufficient control or discipline so that he can profit from the further guidance which is offered. If a person does not want to improve his behavior, he obviously will change little without outside intervention. If he has distracting emotional problems, he is largely blocked from beneficial development. Moreover, if he consistently lacks personal discipline, he is too often thrust out of situations which offer him good learning opportunities. For example, a child sitting in the corner or in the hall outside the classroom as punishment for misbehavior is not likely to learn much of value. Undoubtedly he will be learning *something,* probably not anything good.

The key to guidance is to understand what a person will work for; everyone has some motivation which can be used to get him to perform properly. But, a word of caution: each individual has some of his own individual motivations, which may well be different from those of his neighbor. The guide must find out what these motivations are, and how strong they are. Then the guide can use these motivations as a basis for guiding the behavior of that person in the way which is most beneficial to the person, to his family, and to the larger society.

Many readers will at first object to the idea of one person trying to guide or influence the behavior of another human being. Such an idea has an unwelcome authoritarian sound to it, particularly when we think of dealing with our friends, relatives, and associates. These persons are at about the same level of abilities, skills, and knowledge as we. We do not like to think of them as puppets, reacting to whatever psychological string someone else has pulled. Perhaps, to admit that their behavior can be shaped by another is to admit that our behavior, too, can be similarly guided or directed. We prefer to think that we make up our own minds, without force from others.

At this point I should emphasize that the subject-persons on whom we can use our psychology can be ourselves as well as others. For example, we can analyze our own behavior to gain insight into its causes, and we can administer rewards and punishments to ourselves in order to guide our own behavior toward the goals we have set. Therefore, the subject-person in this book can also be the person who is the proposed user of the psychological principles, using the principles on himself. In such a case, at least, the application of psychology is clearly both moral and desirable.

Many people fear psychology because it might be too successful; they think that a psychologist will "read their minds," or force them to do something "against their will." They apparently believe that a psychologist does his work in a haunted house late on stormy nights, along with a hunchbacked assistant. In truth, however, the typical psychologist, to my knowledge, prefers to work in pleasant surroundings, with as competent and comely an assistant as he is able to secure.

Psychology is a relatively new science. It studies the behavior of men and animals to discover the reasons for their actions. It uses no supernatural powers of perception and influence. As should be obvious from an examination of our society, we frequently cannot get people to do what we want them to do. In fact, it may never be possible to achieve perfect knowledge, sure prediction, and absolute control of behavior, even with greater advances in psychological science. Actually, some people hope that psychology will never achieve such perfect competence. Nevertheless, we should move in that direction because, as I said, at the present time we are in no danger of knowing too much.

We do accept the fact that we can influence the behavior of another, as well as our own behavior, even if we do not like to admit it. For example, we give help to a person in need. If our friend is an alcoholic, we might try to keep him away from the alcohol, perhaps advise him to join Alcoholics Anonymous. We might even insist on driving him home after a party, or taking away his car keys. Similarly, we might expect this same friend to help us when he can, to advise us about whether the soil in our garden will be better suited for growing peas or carrots, or whether we should invest our money in real estate or bonds. Ordinarily, advice is given with the expectation that it may have some helpful effect on what choice the person will make.

If our level of knowledge and skill is much greater than another's, we may actually feel a responsibility toward helping him. For example, we willingly accept the fact that we actually must make all decisions for an infant and control his environment for him; otherwise he would die. The same is true for a very old or very sick person. As the infant matures, he needs fewer controls and limits, less total guidance, and more freedom to choose his own responses. The continuing growth of the person is a process of his taking on more and more freedom and responsibility, proving each time that he can handle it successfully. The helpful adult gradually loosens the guidance. Later, the guidance begins to take the form of advice, suggestions, and interpretations. The guide provides information as a resource person, a back-up person with information and skill when it is needed. He gives praise or other rewards for actions that are commendable and adaptable. He may criticize or even punish when the person has made a bad response. In a healthy family, institution, or society, each person gives aid when he can, and accepts help when he needs it.

An older, experienced worker would typically give guidance to the new worker. A person with specialized training in some area would offer guidance to a person without such training. The leader of a group would help the members of the group to work together to achieve solutions to problems facing the group. This concept has been used in social service programs like the Peace Corps, VISTA, and Big Brothers. The question for daily living is to determine how we can best help others. Obviously the answer is not always to give as much direct physical and psychological help as we can. We must judge when additional help would make a person dependent upon our help when he could go on to accomplish the task himself.

Informal Study

We develop our skills in making judgments by informal as well as formal study of human behavior. Everyone has some practical knowledge of psychology, learned mainly through direct personal observation and experience. You, the reader, probably know more psychological principles than the average person, because you read books such as this one. I expect to build upon this valuable prior knowledge.

Because we deal with other people every day, we learn about them merely by watching them respond in different situations. We often try to predict in a casual way what they will do in other similar situations. A simple example proves this: Consider what you would expect your friend to say if you report that you have just run over a cat with the automobile. Will he be critical and say, "You drive too fast"? Or will he be supportive and say, "I am sure that you couldn't have helped it"? You have observed the actions of your family and friends in order to draw some conclusions about their personalities and hence about their probable reactions to such situations. This is essentially what psychologists do, but in a more organized way, sometimes with special tools and procedures.

This approach—which is called behavioristic—means that psychologists try to learn about people by studying their behavior, not by trying to "read minds," examine horoscopes, or look into crystal balls. A person's behavior gives the best clues to how he perceives, thinks, and feels, because the way that he perceives, thinks, and feels causes him to behave as he does.

The behaviors that are studied may be so obvious and simple that anyone would be able to observe and interpret them. If John punches Jim in the eye, even a poor observer could note this fact and judge that John was probably angry at Jim. Other behaviors might be so small and hidden that special apparatus operated by skilled technicians would be needed to detect and interpret them. Examples of these would be certain psychological responses like changes in electrical conductivity of the skin—which is the main component of the so-called lie detector test—and tracings of so-called brain waves. These small responses, hidden to the naked eye, are nevertheless part of the total behavior of a person, and thus clues to what he is thinking and feeling.

The judgments and inferences about causes of behavior, based on such evidence, are of course subject to error. For example, even though John punches Jim in the eye, under some unusual circumstances this *might not* mean that John is angry at Jim.

The principles described in *Psychology for Daily Living* can be checked against your own informal observations. Consistency with your own experience and understanding will convince you of the accuracy of the stated principles better than any other evidence I could cite.

Formal Study

It is also possible, of course, to improve one's effective knowledge of psychology through formal study. We can learn about people by reading about what others, so-called experts, have observed and recorded. The course of study that will be of most help in understanding people starts with what we already know, perhaps from only informal study, and then leads us on to learn more. Although the principles of psychology are generally familiar, still most persons need help in seeing clearly how these principles can be applied effectively in everyday living.

Value of Study

Throughout my years of teaching I have often been frustrated by the comments of students—even in psychology courses—who do not appreciate the relevance of general, basic psychology to real problems of daily living. But I vehemently assert that the basic principles and concepts presented in this book are central to all situations that involve people. Even if you are familiar with them, it should still be helpful for someone to remind you of these fundamental facts and principles, which you may not, however, view as applying to some current problem.

The inability of intelligent citizens to understand and use psychological principles frequently amazes me. The following hypothetical instance illustrates a number of cases in my experience. The son of a middle-class family had a bed-wetting problem which progressed beyond mere inconvenience into a health problem when he developed a rash. His parents were alarmed enough to take him to a physician who fitted him with a device which prevented him from getting his body wet, successfully curing the rash. Apparently both parents and physician were concerned only about the physical consequences, not at all about the physical or psychological problems that caused the bed-wetting.

Many persons apparently believe that psychology deals only with things that are not relevant to their personal lives, such as maze learning by white rats or the sexual perversions of humans. True, some psychologists may be particularly interested in rats and others in perverted sex, and others may be interested in both—or in neither one specifically. Psychology is in fact concerned with all behavior. This broad interest naturally includes those acts which are most relevant to each person, psychologist or layman, whether the act is large or small, human or animal, normal or perverted. It is important to note that *no acts are excluded.*

My conviction about the practical relevance of basic psychology is in fact my main reasons for writing this book. After giving talks at meetings on some specific applied problems which were not in my area of special interest, I have several times been rewarded by comments about how relevant my remarks were. For example, several years ago I gave a talk to an association of businessmen, lawyers, and public servants who were concerned with the problems in securing rights-of-way across private property. I had accepted the task with some concern, because, I had asked myself, "What of relevance could a specialist in visual perception, once an experimenter with rats, have to contribute to such a meeting?" As is my custom in such situations, I discussed the simple, basic principles of psychology which are described in this book. After the meeting one gentleman, who had been working in the area for twenty-seven years, commented that he had never heard a more directly relevant talk on the subject!

The above story is not told to imply that I have some special knowledge of or insight into problems of rights-of-way. On the contrary, it merely shows that a talk on the fundamentals of behavior must be relevant to the many particular instances of interaction among humans. Although situations and persons differ, the same rules apply to the acts. This commonality of principles fortunately often allows behavioral scientists to simplify the explanations of behaviors of different people in different situations. To be sure, however, the people and situations are often different enough so that the differences must be taken into account, as will be discussed in the next chapter.

The above discussion points up a usual distinction between basic or pure research, from which basic principles are discovered, and applied research on practical problems, which is more limited in application. In basic science, the investigator is primarily concerned with understanding how people come to produce their behavior. Therefore, he studies the general case, selecting from all of the many possible inputs and other factors which can influence the behavior of the persons in his study those which give him the clearest picture of how people function. In doing so, however, he necessarily reduces the number of specific true-life situations to which his results apply directly. Basic knowledge applies only to those situations which are relatively similar to the investigation conditions.

The applied researcher, on the other hand, studies an environment which is as much like the true-life situation as he can reasonably make it. His results will be more practical, but they may only be relevant to the specific conditions involved in his studies. Such studies are conducted because the practitioners need urgently to find answers to practical problems for the benefit of a particular person or a group of persons in a real situation which confronts them *now*. Some problems cannot wait for a solution until all of the basic research is completed, possibly many years later.

The above distinction is only relative, however. Basic principles derived from so-called pure science are also practical, because the more basic the principle, the broader the application to a wider range of different problems. Whereas a specific answer applies only to the particular practical question, the discovery of a basic rule can lead to applications in many problem areas. Therefore, basic research is more efficient over the long run, because it enables us to understand more about the behavior of persons in general.

Some persons argue that the science of psychology provides for no more effective prediction and guidance than could be accomplished with simple reasoning alone. Admittedly, when the reasons behind certain acts are discovered, often they correspond to what many people thought they were all along! This is not to say, however, that psychological science is just "common sense." So much the better if rigorous science and casual observations agree! But sometimes the reasons discovered by psychology seem at first counter to "common sense." When people learn the new principles and become accustomed to using them, they become "merely common sense." Thus, when enough people have learned a principle, it is "common," and when they are familiar enough with it, it makes "sense."

I have conceded earlier in this chapter that our knowledge of the causes of behavior is inadequate in view of our high aims. If we concentrate on the positive side, however, we can think of successes for psychological science. We can point to the development of intelligence tests, the specification of beneficial working conditions, and the progress in dealing with social problems. Excellent specific examples of success in the assessment and training of men can be drawn from the preparation of the astronauts for the United States space program. We now take such accomplishments for granted.

Definition of Psychology

The foregoing discussion is important, because many of the criticisms aimed at psychology are due to incomplete and inaccurate conceptions of its methods and subject matter. A person may learn about a particular psychologist who does research only with rats, and erroneously conclude that psychologists are interested only in rats. He may observe another psychologist who studies the content of dreams and erroneously conclude that psychologists only study dreams. These ideas are as false as observing a medical pathologist or surgeon and concluding that physicians are interested only in dead things or in cutting people up.

Is Psychological Knowledge Dangerous?

Is a book such as the present one dangerous because it only briefly introduces a few basic psychological principles and urges their application to daily situations which may be complicated enough to tax the skill of an expert psychologist? The first argument for a negative answer to the above question is that the book should help the reader use more effectively whatever knowledge of psychology he already has. Admittedly, there is some danger, but surely basic knowledge is less dangerous than the alternative—ignorance.

Second, the main thrust of the book is to promote the use of judgment and restraint in the application of psychological knowledge. Thus, the aim of the new information is to reduce the danger of misapplication of the old.

Finally, everyone is faced with the necessity of using psychology, whether or not he is adequately prepared for it. The parent, for example, must daily—indeed almost continuously—make decisions about child rearing that he may not be prepared to make. He *must* use psychology; therefore he should try to use sound psychology instead of groping in relative ignorance. Any addition to his store of knowledge of basic psychological principles should reduce the danger of his trying to use whatever knowledge he has.

Organization of the Book

The organizational plan of this book is to describe first the field of and the proper approach to psychology, and then the specific mechanisms producing behavior. This brief introduction to the field in the first chapter is followed by some general suggestions in chapters 2, 3, and 4 about the proper attitudes and procedures of study to be adopted by the student of psychology. Chapter 2 asserts the necessity for the applied psychologist to understand the principles of behavior and their application, rather than to attempt to use the psychological text as a cookbook of proven recipes for all occasions. Chapter 3 discusses the continuing problem of establishing the proper relation between scientific thought and humanistic feeling, and argues that the scientific study of man does not rob man of his humanity. In chapter 4, a particular orientation to psychological research is proposed.

The next six chapters are organized in terms of the three obvious components in the functioning of any animal or machine—namely, what goes in, what goes on inside, and what comes out. Chapter 5 considers the influence of the physical surroundings of the person. Chapters 6, 7, and 8 deal with what goes on inside the person in terms of three components: chapter 6 describes motivations and emotions, while chapter 7 presents attitudes and perceptions, and chapter 8 discusses the way the final behavior is selected from all of many possible courses of action. In the next chapter (9), the behavior itself is considered. It consists of the acts which the person eventually produces—the final output after the internal psychological processes have operated on the input.

Chapter 10 describes the consequences which follow the person's behavior, the rewards and punishments that he receives according to the desirability of the behavior which he has just produced. The final chapter (11) gives my personal blessing for reading the book all the way to the end, plus some words of encouragement because of the difficulties to be encountered in attempting to understand, predict, and guide human behavior.

Summary

This chapter points out the need for an understanding of the causes of behavior. Our society is not only multiplying in numbers, it also is becoming more complicated. A person has to learn about people in order to get along with them, using informal as well as formal study methods. The present book is intended to be a first step in the study of psychology, bringing together the formal and informal approaches. The book attempts to show how knowledge of basic psychological principles can help to solve relevant problems in life.

2. A Call for Judgment

No book can tell you what is the exactly proper response to make in a particular situation, or precisely how to solve a specific psychological problem, unless perhaps the book was written with particular persons and situations in mind. A book can set forth the principles for adjustive behavior, but the individual person must develop, largely through his own efforts, the good judgment to apply them correctly. After reading this book, you yourself must work out solutions for the best ways to respond to different people in different situations.

This book, or any other like it, cannot therefore be used like a psychological cookbook; working with people is not very much like baking a cake by following the directions in a recipe. For one thing, the cake cannot take itself out of the oven when it wants to; a person can turn his back, or otherwise avoid your guidance.

For another thing, dealing with other people is too difficult to be accomplished by blind adherence to supposedly successful rules or recipes. There are usually no simple, pat answers to psychological problems, as much as we wish there were! The specific solution to a behavioral problem depends upon such things as the type of problem, the existing conditions, and many other factors. Therefore, a psychological patent-medicine approach is not likely to be successful. Worse yet, its use may prevent the introduction of improved methods—or better medicines, for that matter. A superior method might not even be tried, for example, because one method is already in use, even though it is failing.

Interactions

The first important argument against the patent-medicine approach is the fact of interactions among conditions and people. Frequently, when a psychologist is asked about the proper course of action in some particular situation he wisely replies, "It all depends." He means that the appropriate response depends upon the dynamics of the particular situation—the way one set of conditions interacts with another state of affairs. Many specific circumstances must be taken into account before the proper course of action can be selected. The "it all depends" answer is usually the correct one for practical psychological questions when all of the conditions are not specified.

This interaction effect often causes criticism of psychologists for failing to give a specific answer to an important question about a behavioral problem. "It all depends" is somehow not a very satisfactory answer, but it actually is a proper concern for the different multiple causes of behavior and the complicated interactions among these causes. Often psychological quacks seem to know what to do, whereas the reputable psychologist does not. This is a clear example of fools rushing in where wise men fear to tread. The quack cannot appreciate the difficulty of the problems, and thus foolishly can appear to be totally confident.

Psychology, in fact, continually offers principles which seem to conflict with one another, forcing us to decide which principle we will rely on to solve a real problem. Unfortunately, there is no sure way to tell which principles should be given more weight in deciding upon a course of action in a particular situation. Here the person on the spot in the situation must harness his skills, knowledge, and intelligence—his best judgment—to work out an answer.

The best solution is often a compromise or trade-off between two extreme approaches. This means the achievement of the best benefits from two or more possibilities, while minimizing the disadvantages of each. To take an example, suppose the parent wants his child to be independent. He knows that a child must have the opportunity to act on his own at times in order to develop such independence; the child must not be "tied to mother's apron strings." On the other hand, the child who has been given no parental control or guidance in his early years can also become overly dependent because, as a consequence, he has become insecure. He might think, "Parents whom I can control surely cannot be a safe protection against the hazards of the world. Indeed, Mom and Dad must be even weaker than me, if even *I* can control *them*." Thus, the parents must steer a careful course between being overprotective on the one hand and unsupportive on the other. They must watch the child carefully to judge when he actually needs support because he cannot handle a particular problem by himself, and when he can work out an adjustment for himself, even though with difficulty. All of this will probably produce anxious moments for the parents, of course, but that is one of the burdens of being a good parent.

The selection of the proper course of action thus requires judgment. It is not a matter of following a set plan, a fixed program, or a standard recipe in a cookbook! Even on the few occasions in this book in which I have stated a principle without exceptions, occasionally exceptions may be justified because of other good considerations. Consider the following example: I have said that for training a child to make correct behaviors a particular parental rule should always be enforced. But, from the standpoint of showing love and compassion to the child, the overall gain in establishing a good guidance relationship might, under exceptional circumstances, indicate that a relaxation of rule enforcement is in order.

Individual Differences

A second argument against ready-made answers to questions about the reasons for a behavior is that they ignore differences among people. These differences should never be ignored! Individuals are always different, and the differences are usually important. Even if a program is successful for one case, it may have to be adjusted or modified before it can be used effectively for another individual with different problems and coping abilities.

The principle of individual differences is especially important when we consider people who belong to obviously different groups—physical, racial, social, educational, religious, and so forth. For example, physical characteristics are important. The young do not always react like the old, nor the strong like the weak, nor the sick like the well, and so on. Individual experience is also important; the rich do not always act like the poor, nor the educated like the uneducated, nor the first-born children like the rest of the children in the family, and so on.

Obvious further examples can be drawn from the physiological effects of drugs. Medicines and drugs, for example, specify both adult and child dosages. Also, dosages will often be specified in terms of body weight, with the smaller body requiring less of the drug, of course. A notable illustration of the dangers of guessing appropriate dosages for one organism from those effective for another one can be drawn from a study on the effects of the drug LSD on an elephant (West, Pierce, and Thomas, 1962). Using the same formula of dosage per body weight for the elephant as for a cat produced a gigantic dosage which killed the elephant within two hours.

Persons also have similarities to one another. An important similarity is that they have the same type of nervous system and the same organs of the body. Therefore, the behavior which is influenced by these factors shows similarities among people. For example, each person, regardless of other differences, must sooner or later eat and drink in order to live.

People who have had similar backgrounds and experience would be expected to act similarly to one another, but differently from persons with different backgrounds. For example, an Englishman would be expected to eat with the fork in his left hand, in contrast to the American custom. The behavior of different people within a group of similar backgrounds therefore tends to cluster closely about the average or typical behaviors for that group. There is still variation among individuals, however, because no two people ever have exactly the same environment. Even identical twins living in the same house with the same parents do not have exactly the same experiences, if for no other reason than that twin A deals with twin B, whereas twin B must cope with twin A.

Another example illustrates both the similarities and differences within one group of people. Most Americans would eat an apple if it were packed in their lunch, and probably also most of them would eat all of it except the core. Lunch time at our office does, however, illustrate the variability in apple-eating behavior: one person gives his lunch apple away because he hates apples, and two others consume their apples completely, core and all.

This variability of individual behaviors is a key concept in psychology. The task for psychology is to discover the causes of the similarities and differences in effects. We can achieve some satisfaction in this unless we demand perfect understanding and prediction of behavior. In most cases, we can make a satisfactory general prediction of what a person will do in a given situation, if we know the person well at all. We cannot predict each twitch of a muscle, each thought, but we can form an accurate idea of the general tenor of the forthcoming response. In fact, we are confident enough to bet our lives on it almost every time we drive our automobile, trusting that other people will drive predictably, rationally, and within the traffic laws. Consider the case of driving down a highway and observing another car approaching on a side road. We continue to drive along, betting our lives that the other driver will stop before he enters the highway. We are usually, but unfortunately not always, correct.

We also learn which persons among our acquaintances are very predictable and which ones are unpredictable. It is of some advantage to be able to predict that the behavior of John or Mary will be very unpredictable in some particular situation. In dealing with the unpredictable persons, we must be more alert to the possibility of the need for quick adjustive reactions on our part.

Often the variation in the behavior of one person from the typical behavior of the group to which he belongs is really not important. If a person wants to eat the core of his apple, that is his own business and harms no one. Similarly, if one does not like to eat apples, again this does not create a problem of any great consequence. In such cases, we would ordinarily not spend much time and effort discovering why the person behaved differently from most people. In the case of our luncheon group, the person who hates apples does not know why. In the case of the apple-core eaters, one of them does not know why he does it, except that he once saw someone else do it. The other does so because she had a relative who often gave her apples but did not provide a place to put the cores. She solved the problem of what to do with the core by eating it. Incidentally, it is interesting that behavior such as this, which was once useful, is often still shown, even though the original problem which it solved has vanished long ago.

If the unusual behavior creates some real problem, then we do make a strong effort to understand what caused it. For example, I have a small problem because my first-born child does not like nuts of any kind. My daughter will pick the nuts out of brownies, salads, candy, or she will not eat them. Needless to say, many salads and desserts at our house are nutless. The rest of the family, especially me, loves to eat nuts. The reason for this variation in behavior within our family group is easily understood. When our daughter was a baby we never let her eat nuts, and we became upset if she got hold of any; we had been warned that a piece of peanut lodged in a baby's lung could be fatal. When our second child came along, we were not so nervous about all of the possible catastrophes, and consequently left open his pathway to life-long enjoyment of nuts in desserts.

Thus, the key to sorting out similarities and differences among people is understanding what factors of heredity or environment predisposed the person toward taking the action. We must also learn what aspect of the person's total living situation caused the act to be made at the specific time and place that it did occur. Just as we do not need complete understanding in order to enjoy some success in predicting behavior, the same is true for modifying behavior. Of course, the more we understand, the more effective we can be in producing beneficial changes.

Because it is easier to know about general group characteristics than about the characteristics of individual members of the group, it is easier to understand the average responses of the group than it is to understand why a particular individual in the group responded as he did. Moreover, the best course of action to guide the average person within a group will in all probability not be exactly the best course of action for guiding all of the individual members of that group.

For prediction of the behavior and the guidance of a particular person, therefore, it is best to know and to understand as much about that individual as possible. The college students call it trying to "psych out" the particular professor in order to know why he acts differently from the other professors, so that they may be able to predict what kind of questions he will ask on the test, how difficult he will make the assignments, and so forth. If we cannot understand why some person acts the way he does, our best basis for future prediction is just what he did in similar previous situations.

Normal Variation of Behavior

Fortunately, we can make a general statement about the way a group of people exhibits variations in similarity and dissimilarity. This description can readily be illustrated by a graph. A graph is merely a drawing which illustrates how an increase in one thing is associated with an increase or decrease in something else. The typical graph which describes the variations among individuals is frequently called the "normal curve."

Figure 2-1 is a simplified graph of a normal curve, illustrating the way different persons in the same situation differ in their responses. Whatever the act is, and whatever the measure of responding strength used, we usually expect to find this same picture of the variations among individuals. As is conventional, the horizontal scale represents continuously increasing strengths for some behavior which occurs in a given situation. The behavior might be measured in several different ways. For example, at a track meet we might measure in terms of length—the height of the high-jump bar or the distance of the shot put, or in terms of the time required for running the 100-meter dash. In other situations, we might record the number of kilometers the housewife walks in a day, or how long it takes our dog to start eating a new brand of dog food. We might measure the amount of sweating a paratrooper does before his first jump, or how heavy a load a particular horse can pull.

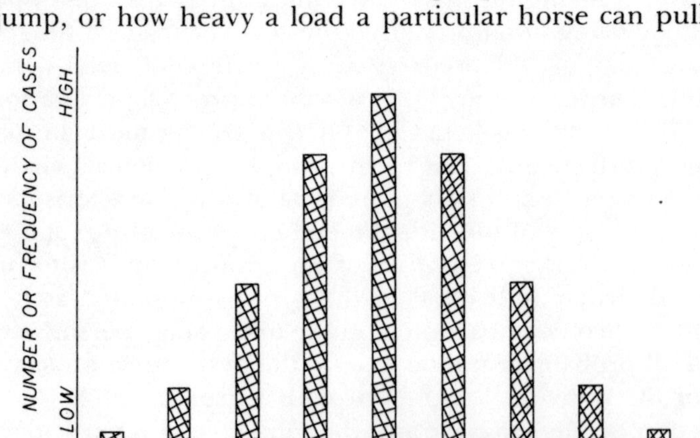

Figure 2-1. Graph of the bell-shaped normal curve showing frequencies of persons with nine different strengths of the act.

The vertical dimension in figure 2-1 represents the number of instances in which each strength of the act occurred, its frequency. This scale starts from a zero point at the bottom and increases continuously until the largest value is reached. The relationship between particular strengths of behavior and the frequency of cases exhibiting each strength of behavior is given by the height of the bar, which of course corresponds to a frequency value on the vertical scale. It is apparent in figure 2-1 that the bar of greatest height, indicating the largest number of cases, corresponds to a medium degree of strength for the act. Fewer and fewer people exhibit strengths of acts of the progressively higher or progressively lower values. For example, relatively few adult high-jumpers can jump over 2 meters, and few can clear only 1.5 meters.

To simplify figure 2-1, only nine bars were used, spaced apart. Obviously, whenever the horizontal scale is continuous, there can be some persons showing strengths of acts at positions between the values represented by the spaced bars in figure 2-1. Figure 2-2 shows what would be expected if the number of persons showing intermediate strengths of behavior were also counted. The heights of these additional bars tend to fall on a smooth line with the tops of the nine original bars, which are the ones shaded in this figure. Because more strengths of response are represented, no space at all is left between the bars. If the individual bars are now made progressively narrower, while at the same time more bars are added so that there are still no spaces between them, then the solid curve gradually loses the stair-step appearance. The final outcome would then be the smooth curve which is also drawn in figure 2-2. In this case the height of the smooth contour above each strength of the act gives the number of people who would be expected to exhibit that strength of act.

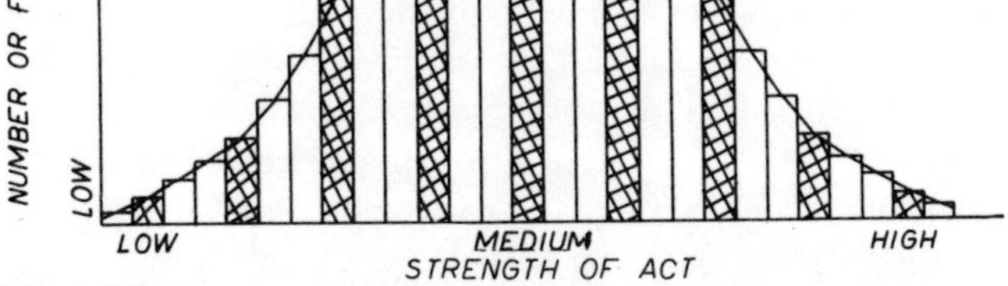

Figure 2-2. Graph of the bell-shaped normal curve showing frequencies of persons with twenty-seven different strengths of the act. Also shown is the smooth curve generated as the number of act-strength categories is increased many times.

The curve in figure 2-2 can be precisely described by a mathematical curve which has several very important properties. One is that it never descends to zero on the vertical scale, no matter how high or low the values of the horizontal scale extend. Because the values on the vertical scale never fall to zero, although they obviously get smaller and smaller at the extremes of the horizontal scale, theoretically there is never a strength of act so low nor so high that some person might not achieve it. Therefore, in theory, no strength of act is impossible for some person to achieve, no matter how unlikely it may be.

You would not expect the results from testing an actual group of people to be as smooth as the graph in figure 2-2. Nevertheless, the results have so often shown this general shape of curve that we ordinarily expect the results of testing a large number of people to look about like this. It is to this normal curve that students refer when they ask the teacher to "curve the grades" on a test. They want the teacher to plot a distribution, such as the one shown in figure 2-2, showing the frequencies of the scores on the test. Each test score is the measure of the strength of the behavior (the learned habit) for the person it represents. From the graph the teacher can get a summary picture of the performance of the class and of each student in relation to the rest of the class. He can get an idea of whether his usual standards for grading the class are too high or too low—that is, whether he expected too much or too little from the class. If the average score for the class is very low, and no student achieved the highest possible score, the teacher might decide that his original expectations were too high; the test was too hard. He might then shift to a relative standard of grading, so that the students achieving the highest scores in the class receive top grades even though their performances were not up to the teacher's original standards.

The graphs in figures 2-1 and 2-2 also can illustrate the results from many responses by a single person in a given situation. The vertical dimension again represents the frequencies with which a given strength of the act was shown by that person. For example, a shot putter will on some days toss the shot farther than on other days. Usually the distances of his tosses tend to cluster around a value which is typical for him—his normal shot put. This cluster of values illustrates what is known as the central tendency of behavior. One way to measure this central tendency is to calculate a mean, or average. This is, of course, obtained by merely adding up all the distances achieved on a number of attempts and dividing this total by that number of attempts. The normal curve shows that those shot puts which are closer to the putter's average are more frequent than those puts that are far above or far below his average. Another shot putter may exhibit a different average but still show the same typical shape of variation for his efforts.

Similarly, a housewife may walk a few more miles on some days than on others, but still over the course of a year show a typical distance covered most often during a single day. If we know what the distribution of the daily distances of walks on, say, Monday—washday—is for the housewife over the course of many such days, then we can make a well-founded confident prediction about the distance that she will walk next Monday—or any given washday. The distance will probably be close to the the cluster of distances that are most frequently covered by her on that type of day.

The housewife will probably not cover a greater distance next Monday than she has ever travelled—but she could. She will probably not cover a shorter distance than she has ever exhibited before—but she could. The mathematical properties of the normal curve make it possible, in such a situation as described above, to make a precise statement of the chances that the housewife tomorrow will walk a distance falling between any two given distances. But notice that we are always dealing in probabilities—the number of times out of 100 chances that something will happen. Consequently, there is always a possibility of being wrong, with a very large error, no matter how confidently the prediction is made. The reason for this has already been given in the discussion of figure 2-2. Because the mathematical curve of the normal distribution never decreases to zero—no matter how high or how low the horizontal scale extends, there is always the real possibility that the person will produce a much stronger or weaker response relative to his usual behavior, and even stronger or weaker than he has ever produced before.

The distances travelled per day by the housewife may also vary according to conditions which are beyond her control. For example, if the weather is very hot, she may not walk as much. If she has house guests, she may have to walk more. Therefore, knowledge of the habitual routine for a given day plus any additional relevant information would help in making a prediction about how far she will walk on that day.

Other Obstacles to Understanding

The science of psychology has some peculiar problems because the object of study and the investigator are both living beings. The total personalities of both must be taken into account, along with the changes in the conditions of investigation. Therefore, a report of what is happening may be incorrect because of the investigator's misperception of environmental conditions, of internal conditions of the subject person, or because of his own personal biases.

A meaningful and useful measure of a psychological attribute must have a sufficient degree of each of four interrelated characteristics: objectivity, reliability, standardization, and validity. Objectivity—the opposite of subjectivity—means that the conclusions are determined by the facts of the situation, rather than by the investigator's personal temperament, biases, or emotions. If characteristics of the test administrator, rather than those of the person taking the test, determine its outcome, then we obviously learn little about the test taker from examining the test results. The existing information tells us instead about the test administrator.

Reliability means repeatability—the degree to which the same result would be obtained if the measurement were repeated. If a person takes a test many times and achieves quite different scores each time, then the test is influenced by (measures) things other than a basic characteristic of the person you are trying to assess, which presumably is not fluctuating. Relatively small "normal" variations are of course always expected, as described above with respect to the normal curve.

Standardization refers to the establishment of the fixed conditions of measurement and to the identification of the population of persons to which the results apply. This is most important in the interpretation of what the test result means. The score of the subject-person can be compared to the standardization, or reference, population in order to determine the relative position of his score with respect to the rest of the scores of the persons in the group taking the test. Is it above or below average, for example? Or what percentage of the persons in the reference population made scores lower than his? This value of the percentage of persons in the standardization group who made a score equal to or lower than a given person is called his *percentile rank* on the test. Usually test results are reported in terms of percentile ranks, because this is more meaningful than the actual score on a test.

Validity refers to the degree to which the proposed measure actually measures what it was intended to measure and purports to measure. This is the most important quality of a good test, or measure of behavior. The measurement or test may be reliable, objective, and standardized, but still not valid. On the other hand, if valid, it most certainly is reliable, and it very probably is also objective.

Each of the above four characteristics is neither, however, completely present nor completely absent. Each may show some degree of variation between a complete manifestation of the characteristic to a complete absence of it.

Environmental Changes

Even though a test may be perfectly valid, the results from a person may change from day to day because the person being studied is not always in the same psychological environment. Each day he is experiencing factors which might change him in important ways. These changes may result from responses to small cues in the environment of which the investigator himself may in fact be unaware; he may unknowingly give cues which affect the performance of his subject. An unintentional half-smile, half-frown, or slight edge on the voice may have a very strong effect on the actions of another.

It may not be what is said, but exactly how it is said, that matters. For example, try repeating six times the sentence, "I never said he stole money," accenting a different word each time. The result is six different meanings. Thus, the perceived attitude of the speaker can be more important than his exact words. The expression, "Smile when you call me that," illustrates this point. My father was fond of telling about his observation of two sailors who obviously were happily greeting each other for the first time in many years. Good friends, they began good-humoredly calling each other by unmentionable names, heaping insults on one another. Undoubtedly, the same words exchanged between strangers would have been cause for battle.

Changed Internal Conditions

The person also responds to internal conditions—ideas, moods, appetites—of which the investigator may be unaware. When the person knows that he is being observed and studied, he often acts as he thinks he is expected to act. He may in fact be unable to act "naturally." Consider the job applicant meeting the prospective boss for the first time, or the schoolteacher conducting a class on parents' visiting day. The story is told about the centipede who could walk quite effectively until someone asked him how he could manage to walk with so many pairs of legs. Therefore, the self-conscious subject probably will not be able to respond as effectively as usual. But, on the other hand, he may be able to get himself "up" to making a superior performance under unusual circumstances, as for a "big game" or an important qualifying test.

These changed internal conditions may be physical or psychological. The ordinarily "good-humored" friend might be rather short-tempered if he has just been insulted or frustrated. He might not want to have a friendly chat if he is sick to his stomach or worried about money. The usually eager spouse might not want to make love if he is too tired or has some physical or psychological problem.

Researcher Biases

The third problem in studying behavior is that the personal wishes and biases of the investigator tend to influence what he observes. This would mean that the behavioral assessment lacked objectivity. What the observer thinks he sees in the behavior of others may be something that he manufactured in his own mind. For example, he is more likely to avoid reaching a conclusion that he does not like than to reject one that he prefers. Similarly, he is more likely to see a disliked person making the error than a person he likes. This tendency to see only good deeds of "good" people is called the "halo effect."

Conclusion

The application of psychological principles is both easy and difficult. On the one hand, each principle taken by itself is relatively simple. On the other hand, many problems in effective use of these principles in complex practical situations have been pointed out. Therefore, the practitioner of basic psychology, who would apply it to daily problems, should be both confident enough to attempt to use psychological principles, but cautious enough to look for and recognize his mistakes.

Summary

This chapter discusses the need for judgment in applying the basic principles of psychology to practical situations. It emphasizes that a book on psychology cannot be used like a cookbook to apply proven general recipes to specific problems. It argues against the memorization of rules or "canned" answers because, first, changes in situations change the way in which the various principles apply, and, second, there are important individual differences among people. Individual differences are represented by the normal curve of performance.

Three problems for understanding that are peculiar to psychology were discusssed. First, the subject-person may be responding to cues in the environment which are not known to an observer. Second, the internal conditions of the person may change, unknown to the student of his behavior. Third, the judgments of the researcher, presumably about the subject-person, may in fact be distorted by his own wishes and biases.

3. Science and Humanism

This chapter compares and contrasts the roles and goals of the scientist and the humanist. Briefly, the scientist focuses his attention on the causes and mechanisms which produce particular behavior, whereas the humanist emphasizes moral and spiritual values which give man his human qualities, his humanity.

Unfortunately, many persons worry about a supposedly unresolvable conflict between science and humanism, although such a conflict does not exist. They fear that the scientific study of man robs us of our concern for human beings, causing us to consider man merely as an object of study. One newspaper article reported that 76 percent of the respondents to a questionnaire, submitted to over fifteen hundred American households, believed that progress in science has gone far beyond our capability in managing our human problems, and that we should start concentrating on the "human side." After the launching of the first Sputnik space capsule by the Soviet Union, Americans suddenly became concerned because our young people had been avoiding the study of science. According to several newspaper articles soon after Sputnik was launched, American high school students considered scientists to be geniuses without moral standards. The purpose of this chapter is to contradict this belief that science is incompatible with humanism.

This public concern about possible conflicting goals between science and human values is the most serious obstacle to the effective use of psychological principles, in my opinion. We must convince society that a person can be at the same time both a scientist and a humanist—that he can in fact use his science to advance human welfare. Science is not the enemy of morality.

It does not seem logical to me that anyone who would read this book would doubt the value of a science of human behavior. But occasionally even students in my psychology classes have objected to a scientific approach toward understanding and guiding behavior. This is an interesting paradox. Perhaps the reason for it is that, as a psychologist friend of mine once said, "We feel as though we ourselves are governed by free will, while we act as though everyone else were controlled by external forces." Freedom of the will means that a person is free to choose in any situation which act he will do, independent of external controls.

Free Will and Determinism

The question of whether or not man has free will is more a philosophical and religious issue than a psychological problem. The only crucial issue for the science of psychology is whether or not there is *complete* freedom of the will. Completely free will would mean that a person would have unrestricted choice of possible behaviors; acts would not in any respect be determined by either internal or external causes. In that case, there would be no way for one person to predict, much less influence, what another would do in any situation.

A friend of mine had a student in his psychology class who attempted to prove that he had free will by writing a nasty word on the chalkboard after class. The psychologist was unconvinced, however. In fact, this act was taken by the professor as further proof that the student had a strong motivation to prove his free will which drove him to perform the antisocial act. Apparently driven to desperation by the psychologist's doubt, the poor fellow went out to the main street of town and took off all of his clothes. Again, the psychologist wondered what drove the student to do this. Such strong motivation actually narrows the range of different acts which might be produced and thus allows the psychologist to predict the acts with some improved degree of accuracy.

Nevertheless, the psychologist cannot disprove free will any better than he can prove it.

Requirements of Science

The behavioral scientist cannot believe in complete freedom of the will, because, if he did, there would be no point in trying to understand the causes of acts. If the behavior of a person in a given situation is entirely unaffected by previous causal events, then it is unpredictable and also uncontrollable. The incentive would be scant indeed to look for behavioral laws and principles which presumably do not exist.

But, on the other hand, a scientist need not believe in complete determinism—the total absence of free will. The behavioral scientist *can* deny the existence of any free will at all—but he does not *have* to. As long as the scientist believes in at least *some* degree of determinism, he has something to study. He can then believe that there are some causes of behavior which can be discovered and understood by his scientific approach. At the same time he can believe that some measure of free will is present, such that he will never be completely able to predict or control behavior.

Choice Not Necessary

I have argued that a person can believe at the same time in both free will and determinism, provided neither position is taken to the extreme. It is a matter of personal choice for each individual to decide what he thinks is the relative importance of free will and determinism in producing human acts. The problem is not to make a choice of Science *or* Humanism—determinism *or* free will. We may choose Science *and* Humanism. One can believe in a limitation on the degree of freedom in "free will," coupled with limitations on the degree of determinability in "determinism."

Evaluation of the Free-Will Conception

The free-will conception has, to my mind, both an advantage and a disadvantage in terms of the personal relationships between people. The disadvantage comes because it is difficult to forgive a person for an unwelcome act—say, a personal insult—if you assume that the act represents a deliberate, free choice by that person. If, however, the act is attributed to some personal problems which cause the other person to act badly in spite of his good intentions, then the injured party can react in a more understanding and sympathetic way.

Also, it would be difficult even to choose a friend if you could never count on what he would do next. If he would act like a friend on one occasion and like an enemy on the next, it would not be easy to behave toward him consistently.

The concept of free will, on the other hand, also has a necessary social advantage. We need a conception of free will in order to develop a social conscience and to promote social justice. If a person performs a criminal act, or some other antisocial behavior, logically we should not punish him if this behavior was determined (driven) by forces that he himself could not control. As a matter of fact, for certain classes of persons, such as the very young or the severely mentally ill, we may consider that they were not responsible for certain of their acts. Consequently, we provide help and treatment for them, instead of punishment.

Scientific Study of Man

Science is merely a search for and a compilation and interpretation of facts about nature. Man, as part of nature, is thus an obvious subject for scientific study. The psychologist studies all of the properties of man, including those that make man different from the lower animals. Some of these characteristics of human beings, such as possession of the most complex brain, are easily observed and verified by the methods of science. Thus observable, they become facts, generally agreed upon by all scientists. Science is based on observable events rather than on meditation from an armchair; it resolves differences of opinion by observing what happens in the natural world.

Nature of Man

Man has a property which is unique to him, and which makes him to a degree different from other animals. This humanity of man cannot, however, be studied by the methods of science. How would it be defined and measured so that science could identify and study it? If we try to devise some objective measure of the humanity of man, we will always find ourselves in a blind alley. An example of this can be taken from an old legal case. The question was whether or not an American Indian was a person, and thus entitled to certain legal rights. The question was decided on the basis that persons could cry, whereas animals could not. Because Indians could cry, they were judged to be persons. This logic has merit, but I doubt if many of us would want to reduce our humanity to this single indicator. Would a person born without tear ducts be less human than the rest of us?

To be sure, as I said, the physical and behavioral sciences have discovered ways in which man differs from lower animals. But to equate any of these differences with the attribute of humanity is, in my view, not proper. The study of this property of man belongs to the fields of philosophy and religion. The scientist, *as a scientist,* is not interested in it; he is not against humanism, nor is he for it. As a scientist he merely ignores this issue, because science itself is neither moral nor immoral—it is amoral, or non-moral. In truth, the same knowledge of behavioral principles can be used for good goals—to educate and to guide—or for bad—to brainwash and dominate.

Nature of the Scientist

There are times when the scientist is not functioning as a scientist, but as a professional person. During those times he may express his humanism. Though science itself is necessarily amoral, scientists as people are not. Most scientists that I know not only hope to protect the humanity of their research subjects, but they also hope to benefit humanity by the results of their research. I certainly do.

Professional organizations of scientists are also interested in nonscientific, ethical matters. For example, the American Psychological Association promotes very strong principles of ethics for its members.

The 1953 publication of the standards of ethics consisted of 171 printed pages (American Psychological Association, 1953). The up-dating of the principles was by 1977 in the twelfth draft (American Psychological Association, 1977). Specific principles supported by the association deal with protecting the rights of individuals, while others deal with the welfare of society in general. One 104-page booklet, published by the American Psychological Association (1973), concerns ethical standards of research with human subjects. For example, the psychologist must not harm or degrade his subjects of study in any way. Clearly, the organization cares about people.

Guidance of Behavior

Some people argue that scientific knowledge should not be used to change or shape the behavior of another person in any way, at any time. This attitude surfaces in truly unlikely places. I encountered it one summer while teaching a course in educational psychology to prospective teachers. This amazed me, because most of us teachers think that we are paid to change people—to make them better persons if we can. The argument for nondirection and nonguidance goes something like this: the teacher does not try to change a child's behavior, but, rather, sets a good example; if the child chooses on his own to change his behavior by imitating the teacher, the teacher is delighted because the child has exercised his free will in a good way. This conception of the teaching process seems to me hypocritical as well as inefficient. A teacher, parent, or supervisor who uses this philosophy has a ready-made "out" if the subject-person does not respond well, does not choose to imitate the example. The free will of the person, and not the instruction, made him respond poorly. In one sense, the so-called guides cannot fail according to that logic. But, if their goal is to promote a successful, functioning person, they obviously fail when the person does not achieve it. Moreover, if the child's free choices are as valid as the teacher's, why send him to school? If the worker is completely free to select his own actions, why give him a supervisor?

In truth, however, any person in an important relationship to another person will cause changes in behavior, whether he wants to or not. As will be fully discussed in chapter 10, behavior followed by a reward is likely to be repeated, whereas punishment will tend to decrease that behavior. *Whether or not a person intends it,* his actions can be interpreted by others as rewards or punishment to them. Thus, it is better to give such rewards and punishments consciously, for carefully selected goals in the best interests of the person, than to mold his reponses in an unknowing, unthinking, haphazard way, merely hoping for a good result.

Some people are so concerned about exerting freedom of will that paradoxically their behavior is completely controlled by others. The two-year-old, for example, often says no even before he finds out what you want from him. Using this characteristic to control the child in reverse is not recommended, however, because it guides him to do the opposite of whatever is suggested. While there may be some apparent short-term gains with this approach, sooner or later it will obviously lead to real grief. Fortunately, most children eventually outgrow this frustrating habit. A few others never do. Any suggestion that he should make some specific response causes the negativistic person to eliminate that as a possible response. Thus, in a backwards way, his behavior is being directly controlled by other persons.

The science of psychology can help to remove internal restrictions on the freedom of a person to perform certain acts. For example, a person may have irrational fears that prevent him from taking some actions. A boy might not ask for a date because he is afraid he will be rebuffed. A worker may refuse a promotion because he fears responsibility. A person may not let himself relax or take a vacation because he has an all-powerful drive to succeed in his job. Some therapy could restore the freedom which was available in external reality but which the person could not enjoy because of self-imposed restraints.

Because man lives in a society of other men, he must establish limits on the permissible acts of each man in order to prevent his behavior from infringing on the rights of another. Therefore, no one is completely free from external constraints. As a colleague once said, "You can only have complete freedon if you do not want anything." It seems to me that true freedom implies an acceptance of this limitation, so that one does not want to commit acts that limit the freedom of another. True freedom is a state of mind that comes about when the well-adjusted man can perform any act that he desires because he does not want to do anything that will harm others or interfere with their rights.

Humanity of Science

Scientific and humanitarian approaches can supplement one another in order to achieve practical goals most effectively. For example, John Dewey, the great philosopher and educator, in his book *Problems of Men* (1946), called for cooperation between scientists and the educators in the schools. He pointed out that the sciences had gained a place in the curriculum, but that they were still mainly separated as a special body of facts, instead of having a central role in providing creative scientific intelligence in connection with any subject. He concluded that the science and philosophy of education should work together to overcome the split between theory and practice which harms both education and society.

We are foolish if we fail to use the tools that science has provided for improving and developing the capabilities of those we would guide. Refusing to use such tools would be like a surgeon declining to use his knife because the incision will cause discomfort, or because the knife in the wrong hands can be harmful. The knife is only good or bad inasmuch as it is used as a weapon or as an instrument of healing. Anatomical knowledge and surgical training for the healer using the knife can only be helpful to the patient.

Giving guidance to another person does not mean that one is forcing the other to act against his will. Certainly no decent person favors heartless control of another human being for personal profit or pleasure. Complete control of another is not advocated here, except in the case of very young children, very old persons, and others who for one reason or another are not competent to make their own decisions. *But such complete control of another should not be confused with guidance,* which leaves the person free to make his own choices of behaviors; the influence of the guide merely tends to help him make the adaptive and helpful response. This book is about guidance.

The behavioral scientist merely wants to discover how different behaviors are produced. Then the knowledge may be used in order to help a person develop behaviors which are appropriate and beneficial to him. The practitioner—therapist, counselor, teacher, parent, or other guide—can thus become an enabler, not an enforcer, of desired behavior. He can help a person to develop a personality that will be free of psychological constraints which interfere with his healthy and happy adjustment to life.

A true story about the behavior of an animal other than a human will illustrate the value of understanding in the guidance of behavior. Some months ago a kitten appeared in our yard. She was very thin and eagerly ate the food placed by the back door. Although she seemed starved for affection, rubbing her body against our legs when she could, she was very fearful and refused either to enter the house or to allow herself to be picked up. It was important for her to overcome this fear because we would not want to keep a pet with such fears.

We concluded that the kitten behaved as she did because of some unpleasant events in her past. Perhaps she had previously been trapped in a house and badly treated, perhaps by young children. We began a therapy for her fears, based on psychological principles discussed in this book. First we built her trust in us by feeding her well, by talking to her gently, by stroking her when she came to our feet, and especially by being very careful not to frighten her. As she gained confidence in us we tried in slow stages to get her to move toward the desired behavior, but always we were careful not to force her. If she wanted to be put down, we did not try to hold her. We left the door open when she finally came into the house, permitting her to see a clear, safe exit. Gradually, she began to allow herself to be picked up and petted, and to purr when let into the house. One day she cried to be let back into the house when I put her out before going to work. Later she began to dart in when the door was opened, and to resist being put outside. She is now another "spoiled" cat, ruling the house just like our previous ones.

It may be argued that some persons do not need training in behavioral science because they have a natural knack for understanding and getting along with people. True, some persons do have such a natural talent. They may be able to do an acceptable—or even superior—job with no psychological training at all. Perhaps a person could also perform successful surgery without thorough training. Does it follow that a person with such talent should therefore skip the appropriate training? No, because an unusual amount of special talent can still be developed, directed, and improved by special training and study.

E. R. Guthrie (1942), a leading theorist and researcher in the psychology of learning, made the same point. He maintained that training in psychology will not make good teachers any more than training in organic chemistry will make someone a good cook. But, he added, good teachers can become better through acquaintance with the general psychology of learning, because a sound psychology furnishes the rationale for good teaching.

Of course, the scientist must not let humanistic considerations influence his judgment in matters of science. He must try to be discriminating and reasoning, rather than careless and emotional, in his scientific work. He must avoid questions of personal values when a scientific decision is to be made. Although the scientist is entitled to his personal opinions and judgments about value, he must make a clear distinction between those occasions when he is evaluating scientific evidence and when he is making a moral decision. Thus, scientists, as responsible human beings, frequently serve two masters. This dual responsibility is possible, as I have said, because the requirements of the two masters are not incompatible.

Some experts would argue that the principle of overriding importance is the expression of true concern for the other person. Then, the details of, for example, the child-rearing practices will not be too important. Thus, true concern for a person can make up for deficiencies in the mechanics of guidance and discipline. The other person will still be able to know even from the mistakes that the guide cares about him. Probably without this manifest concern the attempt at guidance will fail anyway. This perception, that the guide is concerned about the subject-person's welfare, is necessary for certain rewards, like gestures of approval.

In my opinion, true concern or love for another is shown by a desire to do what is best for that person. Many evils are committed in the name of some other kind of fake love, of course. Probably we have all heard a parent of a spoiled child say, "I just love him too much to deny him anything." Such a parent is very likely to be selfish, lazy, or misguided. Some years ago, the term "smother love" was widely used to refer to this misdirected parental affection. The smothering parent is indulging his own desires in a most harmful way to the child, stunting the development of the child as an independent individual. The psychological powers of such a child when he becomes an adult could be as ineffective as the bound feet of a noblewoman in ancient China. Such parents may, in fact, not be too lazy to bother with the demands of giving the necessary training to the child, but rather just afraid of losing the child's affection. Nevertheless, as the Scriptures say, "He that spareth his rod hateth his son, but he that loveth him chasteneth him betimes (Proverbs 13:24)."

As we have seen, love alone, without the proper behavior which comes from understanding, will not be effective in developing the proper acts. According to my conception of true concern, the actions will be the natural result of the desire to discover and to do what is best for the other person. Conversely, the self-lover will not bother with either. In my opinion, the do-gooder who "wants to help people" but does not want to bother with learning enough to provide the effective help, is grossly irresponsible and a hypocrite. The familiar advertisement for dog food, "All you add is love," does not really hold true even for dog foods. It is always necessary to add a little judgment about when, and how much, to feed the dog. If you truly love your pet, you will study how to take care of dogs, so that you can best take care of him. You will learn how much food he should have, and you will not over-feed him even though he begs for more food.

The personal concern may, however, cloud the judgment of the person so that he cannot see certain problems, or bring himself to take certain necessary steps. Therefore, the person must always ask himself whether he is actually doing something for the good of another or for his own personal comfort. As we will see, it is not easy for us to know whether or not we are being selfish when we bestow gifts, or when we deny them. The person with true concern will make the effort to find out, by securing outside counselling help, for example, if this is necessary.

Summary

The main argument of this chapter has been that there is no necessary conflict between the requirements of science and those of humanism. The scientist does not deal with humanistic problems in the conduct of his science, but he often is concerned with such problems as an individual professional person. The objections of some people to a science of psychology seem to be caused by emotional barriers, or by a failure to understand the nature of science. Science merely provides the method, the tools, to reduce the errors that often accompany subjective judgments.

This chapter also argued that it is morally defensible to influence or guide the behavior of another person. True concern for the welfare of another will result in acts aimed at guiding that person toward behavior which will benefit him. Also, study of psychological principles is moral because it will make the guide more effective in giving such guidance. It is pointed out that free will is not necessarily an all-or-nothing proposition; there may be limited freedom of the will, with appropriate, correspondingly limited determinism.

4. A Way of Understanding

The purpose of this chapter is to discuss a way of thinking about people which helps in understanding the causes of their behaviors. Although the approach which I propose is of course not the only possible one, I find it the most useful to me. It emphasizes the need for an analysis of inputs, both present and past, and other existing conditions in order to determine how the various acts are produced. This analytic approach assumes that a person's acts are determined by many factors, such as his knowledge, experience, emotional state, motivation, and physical capabilities. Therefore, he may not exhibit appropriate behavior in a given situation because of problems with any or all of these factors.

Knowledge of the facts and circumstances which cause the behavior can help the guide to select an appropriate course of action to improve an outcome. Once the reason for a wrong act is discovered, then a solution for correcting it is probably very close. As Dr. Wernher von Braun stated after the Apollo 13 accident, the only real problem facing the scientists and engineers was to discover what went wrong.

The cause of a person's behavior is not always easy to discover, of course, because some acts are seemingly quite contrary to known psychological principles. Take as an example the case of the child who misbehaves to get attention. A schoolteacher described to me certain children in her class who actually wanted to be spanked. Because they belonged to a family with eleven children, discipline was about all their mother had time to give them as an expression of her love and concern. The children understood that she would not spank them if she did not care for them. The gain of attention was more important in influencing their behavior than was the pain from the spanking. After the cause of the problem was discovered, the way to stop their misbehavior became obvious: the teacher gave the children attention for good, rather than bad, behavior.

Methods of Study

The analysis of causes of behavior uses the three general methods of science: naturalistic, correlational, and experimental. The investigator can use any one of these techniques by itself or in combination with either of the others.

Naturalistic

The naturalistic method is merely to observe behavior and the environmental conditions which preceded and accompanied it. For example, the researcher would collect as much information as he could about a mentally ill person, including facts about his current life situation, his family history, and important events in his past life. From this he would make a judgment about what events or conditions might have caused the illness.

Correlational

The correlational method examines the relationships among selected physical, psychological, and behavioral events. An example of this would be to discover whether or not there was a relationship between students' grades in high school and their success in college. A correlation between two such events could mean that one caused the other, because the causal event consistently precedes the caused event, necessarily producing a correlation between them. But all correlations do not necessarily reflect causation; a correlation could occur because both events were themselves caused by some other third factor. For example, a correlation between high school and college grades could occur because the brighter the student the greater the likelihood that he will make good grades in either academic situation. This relationship could however also reflect causation because the better high school preparation could facilitate the achievement of higher grades in college. Detailed analysis of the situation by the investigator would be required before he could conclude whether or not the correlation did in fact represent a causal connection.

Even though an observed correlation does not represent a causal relation between two events, it nevertheless can provide useful information for the psychologist in predicting future behavior. For example, a positive correlation between high school and college grades, regardless of the reason for it, implies that the student making higher grades in high school will probably make higher grades in college than the student who made lower grades in high school.

Experimental

In the experimental method, the researcher changes some input condition for a subject-person and then evaluates whether or not the person behaved differently than he would have if that condition had not been changed. The unchanged condition which is used for comparison purposes is called the "control" condition; it is necessary so that the experimenter can form a conclusion about what the response would have been without the change in conditions. An example of an experiment would be a comparison of work by the same persons tested once in a quiet room (the control condition) and once in a noisy room (the experimental condition). Alternatively, the experimenter could place the experimental subjects in a very noisy room and compare their performance on some task to that of a similar control group of persons tested in a quiet room.

Problems of Studying

The mechanisms inside the person are the most difficult to study because they cannot be observed directly. By using clues and inputs which we *can* observe, we must infer what is going on inside, the unobservable states. The word "clue" is used here just as it is in solving puzzles or crimes. The clue is observable, factual information which hints at or points to a solution, but ordinarily does not itself give the solution directly. For example, the detective in trying to solve a crime gathers as many clues as possible to help him arrive at some conclusion about the characteristics of the criminal. He asks himself what type of person would be responsible for the existing physical evidence. All of the clues put together produce an idea about the characteristics and thus possibly the identity of the criminal. If the detective does not have a sufficiently strong case against a particular suspect, he may then lay a trap for him. The purpose of the trap is to get the suspect to reveal himself by committing further incriminating acts in a situation contrived by the detective.

Similarly, the student of behavior looks for clues in the behavior of a person to help him guess at what the person is like inside. He observes the acts of the person; he notices what conditions were present when the acts were committed. He obtains his most powerful evidence, however, when he does an experiment. Like the detective, he tries to trap the factors responsible for the acts into revealing themselves to him. On the basis of his suspicions or hypotheses about some internal mechanism, he deliberately manipulates some input to the person and observes the reaction. If the new reaction is what the researcher expects, his suspicions about the expected internal mechanism are confirmed. If an unpredicted outcome occurs, the experimenter concludes that his hypothesis was incorrect. For example, if a small baby is crying, his mother might recall that the child has not eaten recently. Consequently, on the basis of her hypothesis that the baby is hungry, she attempts to feed it. If the baby refuses to eat, and still cries, the mother concludes that her original hypothesis about the cause of the baby's behavior is incorrect. She next guesses that the baby is wet, and checks this. If the baby is dry, and still cries, she rejects the second hypothesis, and tries additional guesses. She might in turn check out whether or not the baby is teething, stuck by a pin, sick, cold, or, finally, just crying for attention.

Thus, the person who would guide or help another must carefully observe the effects of his first tentative solution to the behavioral problem. If the desired results are forthcoming, he can congratulate himself on success. If the outcome is still not satisfactory, the guide must reanalyze the situation in order to arrive at another tentative solution, which is then tried. If he fails again, he continues testing different hypotheses until he finds an answer which works. The length of time it takes him to find a workable solution will depend upon how hard he tries, how intelligent he is, how well he understands psychology, and how lucky he is.

The above procedure is ordinarily more difficult whenever the subject-person cannot talk. As a baby gets older, the task of the mother is simplified because she can ask him what is wrong or where it hurts. Unfortunately for mother—and for the student of behavior—the child often cannot, or will not, tell her what the problem is. Similarly, the supervisor or foreman at the factory can ask the worker what is troubling him. But even adults often do not know why they do certain things. Frequently, also, they will not give the true reasons for their acts, even when they do know what they are. A complete and factual reply would in part depend upon the effectiveness of the lines of communication. If the person had reason to believe that anything he said would be held against him, he would naturally be reluctant to speak.

Before attempting to understand the behavior of others, the guide should first attempt to understand himself. If he understands his own motivations and views, he will be less likely to form a distorted view or interpretation of the behavior of others. The student of behavior must keep in mind that he himself also is the victim of the same influences that affect the behavior of the other person; his decisions and conclusions are also affected by his own personal desires and personal views. No matter how intelligent he is, and no matter how persistently he tries to avoid it, he can be misled by his own personal biases and wishes in drawing his inferences.

Before he is able to participate successfully in the guidance of others, the guide must, in particular, rid himself of stereotyped thinking and prejudices. He cannot thoughtlessly assume that another person is wrong merely because he is a member of a different ethnic group, or that he is right because he is a member of his own ethnic group. Each person who is to be guided must be considered as an individual, who should ultimately be understood in terms of his own acts in response to certain inputs rather than on the basis of certain physical or behavioral resemblances to other people. In short, as was explained in chapter 2, a successful guide cannot have pat conclusions and solutions—psychological patent medicines—for use in every situation and for every person.

Person as Machine

The analysis of behavior can be facilitated by considering the person as a special machine. The psychologist tries, by observing the actions of the human machine, to discover how the machine is put together and what internal mechanisms are responsible for its output, or responses. Obviously, some characteristics are possessed only by man, and not by machines.

Input

As with any other machine, the person responds to information which is put into him. By observing what comes out of the machine, and relating it to what is put into the machine, we make some inferences about what is happening inside. For example, the performance of the family automobile is obviously determined by the input to it. The position of the ignition switch, the pressure on the gas pedal, the setting of the gear selector, all control the output of the machine.

The person similarly responds to inputs. For example, his actions are affected by verbal instructions. The parent tells the child to wash his hands before dinner; the officer shouts commands to his troops. The person also follows the directions of visual signals, such as traffic lights and no smoking signs. Similarly, he responds to noninstructive inputs, as by taking off his coat in a warm room or by putting his hands over his ears in a noisy factory.

Internal Conditions

The performance of the automobile is influenced also by its internal conditions. For example, the proper responses of an automobile require gasoline in the tank, a sufficient charge in the battery, a workable transmission, and proper timing of the engine, among other things.

Similarly, the person will not act correctly if he does not have the proper internal physical conditions. He will probably not attempt to high jump if he has a broken leg, nor will he ride on the carnival rides if he is too sick. He will avoid eating ice cream if he does not like it, or if he has already eaten too much cotton candy.

Outcome

When the performance of the automobile is disappointing, we look for the cause in terms of our understanding of the mechanics of automobiles. If the engine will not start, we check to see if the ignition is on, and then the gasoline, the battery, and so forth. If it runs but will not stop, a check of the brakes is appropriate. If the ride is too bumpy, we check the shock absorbers. We must make some guess about the reason for the trouble before we can intelligently attempt to fix the machine or to supply the missing items. Similarly, if the acts of a person are inappropriate, then the interested parent, supervisor, or other guide tries to make guesses about what is wrong. He may blame the input, or something amiss inside the human machine.

The Analysis

The mechanic or interested automobile owner learns about what things are likely to go wrong with a given make and year of car. Automobiles, like people, tend to have "personalities"—or should I say "automobilities"? Particularly as they get older, they will develop actions and reactions that are peculiar to them, depending partially upon how they were fabricated and also upon the experiences that they have been through. An automobile that has been in a wreck may have a bent frame, for example. From observing what this particular machine has done under given circumstances in the past, we gain some correct expectations about how it probably will perform in the future. This is why the car owner likes to have a mechanic who is familiar with his particular car. Similarly, the mother wants to have a family doctor who is familiar with the medical history of the family members. On the basis of his past experience with them, he can predict what ailments they are more likely to have.

We do the same thing in attempting to predict human behavior. Many good examples of this use of psychology can be taken from athletics. The basketball coaches keep a "book" on each opposing player. This is a detailed record of his past performance, giving the relative frequencies with which he has taken shots at the basket from various positions on the court, and what kinds of shots they were. After a player has studied the book on the opposition, he can make accurate predictions about where they most probably will make their shots, and what kind of shots they will be. In football, the quarterback is also likely to settle into consistent patterns, calling the same plays in similar situations, particularly if he has been successful with them in the past. Scouting the opposition in sports is merely using the observational method of science.

All of us show such consistency of actions, or habits of behavior, in our daily lives. People who know us well have learned this about us, and are able to predict our reactions. For example, my wife knows that I want a cup of coffee after every meal, but my mother wants a cup of coffee before every meal, and another half cup before the meal is over. My wife knows that I like to watch football on television, but hate to pay bills, and therefore am more likely to be seated in front of the TV than at my desk. She also knows that the probability of finding me at my desk will be greatly increased if the power company has just threatened me with loss of electrical service for nonpayment of bills. Therefore, prediction of human behavior is very easy in some cases.

Similarities of Man and Machine

The above discussion has identified certain similarities between man and other machines. Both are made up of various parts and mechanisms which influence their acts. Failure of parts to work properly will produce incorrect, nondesired acts. The machine can be structurally modified if it is to be expected to perform some new behavior; the operator does not expect the machine to perform acts which are beyond its physical capabilities. For example, the driver does not ordinarily expect his personal automobile to move sideways, or to achieve a speed of 250 miles per hour.

In the case of a machine, the potential acts are established by the designer and the factory workers. The mechanic and driver jointly determine the degree to which the particular automobile will approach its full potential. Similarly, the child at birth has certain potential psychological and physical abilities. This potential is in the design of the "machine," established at the time of conception in the "blueprint" of his genetic—inherited—background. These potential abilities can be developed and maintained as a result of experience and proper nurture. The goal of society should be to help each person bring his potential capacity to actuality, just as the manufacturer of automobiles tries to implement all of the features in the automobile that the designers had in mind.

The machine can also be modified by experience. Its behavior can be changed as a result of accidental damage or by abuse. For example, we avoid buying a used taxicab because the excessive use and abuse it probably has suffered is likely to affect its future behavior. Even without abuse, the general aging process would affect the behavior of both the machine and the person. Occasionally, a single powerful experience can have a great and permanent effect on the subsequent acts of a person. After once being bitten by a dog, a child may never again like dogs. Having lost a loved one, some persons never let themselves love again.

Differences of Man and Machine

Although the human being and other machines are similar, they are also different in several respects. An obvious difference is that the human being ordinarily cannot easily replace damaged or worn-out parts. Some parts cannot be replaced at all. Obviously, it is not possible to junk the human machine when it is not working properly.

Although the automobile may be changed as a result of wearing out, being wrecked, or by modification of parts, still automobiles of the same make and model tend to be rather much alike. The skilled mechanic, or used-car salesman, could distinguish variations among automobiles of the same make, model and year by examining the frame for evidence of previous wrecks, and other parts for evidence of wear and replacement of parts. One would expect greater differences between persons than between automobiles. This difference is important when one is predicting the behavior of groups of people or the acts of individual persons. Groups of people will behave similarly partly because their experiences will tend to be similar. In the long run, the effects of some abnormal experiences of some members of each group will be countered by different abnormal experiences of other people. A given person may have an "off day" or be "hot" on a given day. But the chances are that all members of the group will not go "off" together. The average result for the groups is determined by poor-performance days of some persons, along with good-performance days of other people. These issues were discussed in chapter 2 with respect to the meaning of the normal curve.

A final difference between man and machine is that the man is thinking and feeling and learning. True, many of the feats performed by man have been duplicated, or even exceeded, by specially built machines. Some scientists believe that all human functions could be duplicated by machine if we just knew how man accomplished them. At present, we do not know enough about these human functions for this. In any case, man must certainly be thought of as the most complex and miraculous of machines.

Society as Machine

In much the same way that we have described the similarities between man and machine, we can point out similarities between man, machine, and the society of man. The conception of a society can be similarly simplified by looking at it as a machine which can be characterized as responding to certain inputs with particular responses. Although the approach and orientation are the same, the actual task may be considerably more difficult.

This interpretation is partly obvious, because society is a collection of persons, and thus the group processes should represent a combination of the individual processes. Just as you would not expect one person always to have at each instant the same prevailing motivation, for example, you would not expect all members of a given group to have exactly the same motivations. You would expect, however, many people of the same group to have similar motivations. Most poor people would tend, for example, to favor increased welfare benefits, even if such increases meant higher taxes for those who were better off financially. The rich would probably oppose the taxes. Politicians recognize this principle very well. While campaigning in rural areas, they emphasize their support for legislation to protect the farmer, and in seaport cities they favor legislation to increase maritime business.

Similarly, the actions of the group are followed by various rewards and punishments. The larger group, as the individual member, would alter its behavior in accordance with the state of affairs that followed its responses. For example, one nation may impose a heavy tax on certain exports to another country, and then quickly repeal it if that country responds by buying the products elsewhere, resulting in less revenue after the tax than before it.

The Effects of Physical Structure

One of the first recorded phenomena of psychological science was the firing of an astronomer's assistant for having differences from his superior in judging the position of stars. The judgments differed because of differences in reaction time between the two men, reflecting a difference in their physical capabilities. Because the astronomer was not aware of such differences among persons in the time different individuals required for making a response, he attributed the differences to the carelessness of his assistant.

As discussed in chapter 2, these individual differences are always important. For example, the physical structure of the body, determined by both genetic inheritance and circumstances such as illness or injury, sets limitations on the possibilities for performance. A child with poor visual acuity might be unable to copy the homework assignment from the chalkboard. A color-blind person might have difficulty responding appropriately to traffic lights. A tone-deaf volunteer creates problems for the choir director. A worker with lower intelligence might have trouble in remembering the shop rules, or in learning to operate a new machine.

Extrasensory Perception

One class of supposed human behaviors, if they do in fact exist, do not obey physical laws. These usually are described under the name of ESP, or Extrasensory Perception. As the term implies, this behavior refers to perception of stimuli by some other than the known sensory receptors. Included in this class of phenomena are reported instances in which persons dream of events happening many miles away, even events to happen in the future. Similar types of alleged behavior are "mental telepathy," or communication directly between minds over great distances. Another alleged phenomenon is P.K. or "psychokinesis," which refers to the alleged ability of a person to use thought to influence the movement of physical objects, such as dice or playing cards.

There is considerable controversy among behavioral scientists about whether or not any of these supposed abilities exists. Without going into the details of the arguments, the proper conclusion at this time, in my opinion, is that there is no conclusive proof one way or the other. The issue probably can never be resolved scientifically. In the first place, we can never prove that a thing does not exist. One can look for that thing in a million places a million times and not find it, but he still does not know that he will fail to find it the next time or in the next place he looks. The problem is like trying to prove that you are not a homosexual or a Communist.

In the second place, the proposed nature of these extraphysical capabilities means that they are not likely to be proved by the methods of physical science. If a means of communication does not obey the physical laws of space and time, how can it be scrutinized by a science which presumes those laws? If we depend upon merely mathematical and statistical arguments, we are again vulnerable, because anything can happen by chance. In any case, even if these unusual capabilities are possessed by certain persons, they are not important for a book on practical psychology. These abilities apparently are not well enough developed or under sufficient control to replace the telephone and telegraph, or to put the gaming tables out of business in the near future.

Physical Limits

Limitations of the responding apparatus of the person would of course restrict the kinds of acts that could be done. The person may not have the physical strength or coordination to perform a certain act. For example, the well-known ninety-seven-pound weakling should not be expected to become an All-American football player. He might make it, but the odds are against it. Similarly, the chances would be slim for a person with an unpleasant speaking voice to become a radio announcer.

The maturation of the physical structure is particularly important in assessing the capabilities of children. As the baby matures, he is able to perform physical acts which were previously impossible for him. For example, we do not expect the newborn child to be able to walk; he must mature some first. The timing of the maturation is extremely important for guidance. For example, the parent should not expect his child to walk or to become toilet-trained until his muscles and nerves are sufficiently mature to provide voluntary control. The teacher should not expect the child to be able to write until his hand is physically mature enough to hold a pencil.

An injury to the person may also prevent him from performing certain acts. It is not always possible for a physician to repair the results of a birth defect or injury; for example, the nerves in the brain do not regrow when they have been killed by injury. This fact must be recognized by parents whose child has such a handicap. They must learn to accept the fact of the damage and then try to find ways to compensate for it. The idea is to develop those capabilities that are present—to train those skills and talents which remain. Tragically, some parents refuse to accept the truth about their child, thus preventing him from getting the special help that he needs to overcome or compensate for his handicap.

Physical maturation not only affects the physical responses of the child, it also influences his mental activities. The child grows intellectually; he becomes able to solve complex problems. He learns new motivations, becomes able to sustain them, and improves in his ability to control his emotions.

The important concept for the guide is readiness. The child must be mature enough physically to be successful in achieving a new act. This readiness does not always occur at the same age in years, months, and days for each child. Some children mature faster than others physically. Thus, the age at which a child begins to walk can easily fall between eight and sixteen months; a few children walk even earlier or later than those extremes. The exact age of walking is influenced by many factors, including such things as the weight of the child and the kind of experiences he is allowed to have.

Psychological Limits

Readiness can also be evaluated in terms of the psychological state. Some children have richer environments which enable them to develop faster intellectually. It is important to keep this in mind when assessing the mental capacity of a culturally disadvantaged child. Although a person may be sufficiently mature physically to attempt an act, he may be unready in terms of past experience or emotional maturity. The boss or foreman should not expect the new worker to be able to keep up with the older, more experienced workers at first. The neophyte may need an orientation or adjustment period, or specific training for a job, and then some period of practice in order to reach their level of performance.

Readiness

Whereas the stages of maturation are reached at different times by different persons, the sequence of these stages tends to be the same. For example, the child learns to crawl before he learns to walk. He can lift his body off the floor before he can crawl. Before that, he gains the ability to hold his head up without support. Thus, the guide can predict what developmental stage will come next, and, by observing the subject-person carefully, about when to expect it.

Thus, the child must be physically, as well as psychologically, ready to perform the acts which are characteristic of a higher stage of development. If certain acts are expected of a child before his physical apparatus is capable of performing those acts, then he and the parent will become frustrated. The parent and teacher must keep in mind that children are not just small adults. They often cannot perform the acts that may be easily accomplished by the mature physical and psychological apparatus of the adult.

Psychological readiness would be of concern in deciding whether the child is mature enough to begin school, or to start dating, or to go away to college. Is the adolescent ready to get married? Is the widow ready to start dating other men, because she has succeeded sufficiently in coping with her bereavement?

Effect of Psychological Processes

The physical condition of the person affects his mental condition, just as psychological factors can influence the physical body. For example, a physically fatigued person is not as likely to be as alert mentally as when he is rested. A worker may not be able to perform up to the requirements of his regular job because he is "moonlighting" on another job, and thus generally tired.

Teachers of disadvantaged children often must contend with behavior problems of their children caused by poor physical condition. For example, the disadvantaged child may live in crowded housing where it is impossible for him to get sufficient sleep and rest. Such a child is naturally more likely to be irritable. Also, he might have diseased teeth, or other untreated illnesses, which pour poisons into his system and make him feel bad and behave poorly. Teachers have told me of very good results from providing a bowl of breakfast cereal for a child who has had to come to school without breakfast, often because there is no money. Those of us who always feel, and act, miserable in the morning until we have had breakfast understand what this is like.

Another instance of the influence of the physical condition of the body on psychological processes can be drawn from sensory processes. For example, excessive heat, noise, or other noxious conditions in the working area could contribute to lower levels of production, along with lowered morale.

Mutual Physical Effects

Particular physical conditions in some parts of the body can affect other parts. An illustration can be drawn from the action of hormones. When the child reaches puberty, the sharp increase of sex hormones influences the development of certain body structures. There is a general growth spurt, along with the appearance of appropriate secondary sexual characteristics, such as broad shoulders in the male and broad hips in the female. These physical changes also influence the kinds of acts that the person can, and will want to, perform. The child begins now to seek the company of the opposite sex, and to perform rituals that he thinks will be attractive to his opposite—like lifting weights or adorning the body with cosmetics.

Implications

The known influence of physical factors on the acts of a person tells us that his physical health should be checked if he is performing abnormal acts; the abnormal acts may merely be the result of some physical problem. For example, a child in school may appear to be inattentive to the teacher when in fact he has a problem of deafness or poor vision. Tragically, some children have even been classified as mentally retarded, when in fact they were deaf.

Interaction with Experiences

The acts that are done by a person are not determined solely by his physical condition and capabilities, but also by the environmental influences to which he has been exposed. As an example, consider the possible results of a predisposition to obesity by someone in our culture. A person who is considered to be overweight is likely to have certain unpleasant experiences which others do not have, like being compared to the "before" picture in an advertisement for reducing aids. If, however, the society considers the ideal weight to be much greater, the "overweight" person would conversely experience favorable reactions and therefore tend to develop a good conception of himself. In some societies, the fat wife is desired, because she would be more likely to survive a famine.

A similar situation would occur for a person who had a glandular disturbance which made him either more or less active physically than the average person in the group. One society might hold the highly active person in high esteem as a "go-getter" and scorn the underactive person as a "lazy bum." A different society might consider the more active person "pushy" and the underactive one "relaxed and friendly." Therefore, the effects of a particular physical attribute depend upon the particular attitudes of the culture in which a person lives. If the physical attribute is looked upon with favor by the persons in the community, he will enjoy more pleasant experiences and rewards and suffer fewer unpleasant experiences. If these experiences shape his personality, can we say that our physical structure determines the kind of personality that we will develop?

Both heredity and experiential influences account for family resemblances, of course. Because members of the same family have similar physical inheritance from their common ancestors, their physical structures would produce similarities of behavior. But members of the same family typically also have similar environments, and therefore similar experiences, which also would tend to produce family resemblances in behaviors. Thus, members of the same family are likely to show similar levels of intellectual capacity because of the joint action of heredity and environment. A given family may apparently produce more than its share of musical geniuses, because musical genius obviously requires high intelligence and certain other physical abilities, which a person would inherit. But a child in such a family would also be exposed constantly to music, and be strongly and continuously rewarded for music-related activities. As we have said, the heredity may set certain limits on the possible level of development of the person, whereas the environment determines the extent to which the person approaches this maximum limit of his inherited capacity.

As the child grows older, new acts may replace some of the old ones. These changes sometimes are a result of the maturation of his physical equipment. We rely on the physical maturation process when we ignore a child's behavioral problem on the assumption that "he will outgrow it." One should be sure, however, that a problem is due to physical immaturity before it is ignored because of this assumption.

Behavioral differences between the sexes can be attributed in part to the differences in physical structure. Men are of course on the average larger and stronger, and therefore more suited for acts which require physical power. Women are in some respects naturally more physically suited for the care of infants. But, of course, many differences in the behaviors of the sexes are caused merely by different roles forced upon boys and girls by society. More and more of these arbitrary boundaries and attitudes are being broken down by education and by law. We are seeing more male nurses, for example, and more women bus drivers, because the sex of the person does not put a physical limitation on his ability to perform such work.

Effects of the Mind

The psychological state of the person influences the body structures, and hence behavior, in many ways. For example, adjustment problems or nervous tension can result in headaches. The business executive develops stomach ulcers under the pressure of his responsibilities, as discussed more fully in chapter 6. Such effects indicate the close relationship between physical and psychological states. Problems of either nature can stem from problems in the other area. The field of psychosomatic medicine recognizes that some physical ailments have psychological causes.

The Information-Processing Diagram

This section discusses a diagram, presented in figure 4-1, which I will use in the rest of the book to aid in explaining the causes of human behavior. This diagram shows an "Information-Processing" model, so-called because it describes how information put or taken into the person is processed or treated and thereby changed in ways that affect his behavior.

The Input

Starting at the left, the input to the person is represented. This is the information in his environment to which he can respond, consisting of

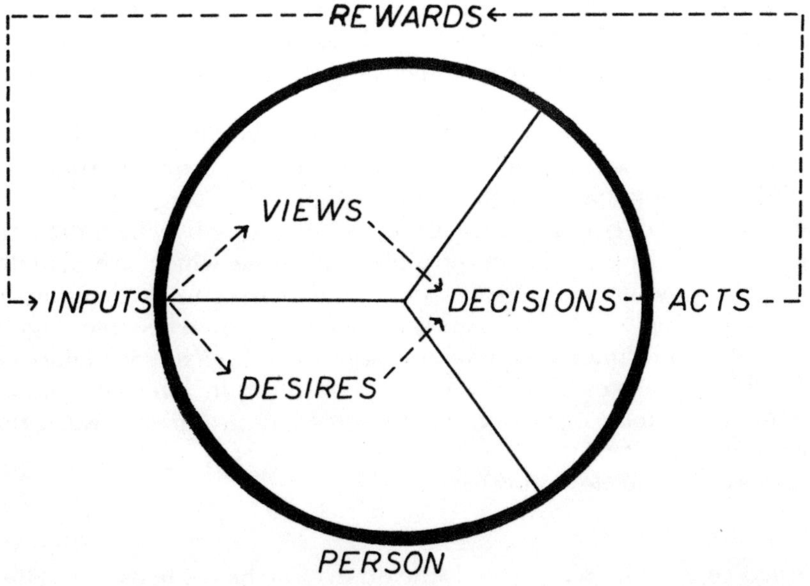

Figure 4-1. Diagram of a simple way to think about what causes a person to act the way he does.

stimuli in his external environment as well as those arising from the parts of his own body.

The Person

The heavy black circle in the diagram represents the person, consisting psychologically of three parts—desires, views, and decisions. Each of these parts can be modified by experience. These internal psychological parts will now be described briefly and later discussed in greater detail in chapters 5, 6, and 7.

Desires The desires refer to the motivational states of the individual. They are, in short, the needs he wants to have satisfied. We make inferences about what he wants by finding out what he is willing to work for, assuming the usual correspondence between the internal state of the person and the acts that he performs. Conversely, we ordinarily assume that a given motivation is not present if evidence for it does not show up in the person's behavior. For example, if a person professes to be greatly concerned about problems of ecology, yet never serves with groups working to improve the environment or develops such projects on his own, we conclude that his motivation in this area is indeed not strong. Thus, actions often speak louder than words in telling us what a person really wants.

Views The views of the person refer to his way of looking at things. Included in this are his attitudes, opinions, and philosophy about everything—politics, religion, education, child rearing, and so forth. For example, we might refer to his views on religion which would influence his responses with respect to such things as churchgoing, contributing to charities, conducting business, and so forth.

Views are, of course, established through learning in many different situations. Thus, a person with different experiences from another person would probably have a different viewpoint.

Decisions The decisions are the processes of choice by which the person selects from the group of possible acts those which are actually performed. Sometimes a person's views and desires work together to produce a decision which favors the same act, which then becomes highly probable. At other times, the views promote an act which may be incompatible with one fostered by the desires, resulting in internal conflict. Thus, the final choice of an act may be some compromise between the conflicting demands of the desires and the views, causing the person to show indecision and hesitation.

The Acts

The acts represent, in figure 4-1, the observable bits of behavior. They are the "pay-off," the final common path of the results from the interplay of all inputs and internal processes. Some are primarily direct responses to input information. Others are primarily the result of the continuous modification of that information by the internal processing characteristics of the person—in short, his personality. Because these internal characteristics have been built up and changed by experiences of the person, his present responses can be in a sense influenced by inputs received many years previously which have left their mark on his habitual way of processing information.

Some acts are easily observable by other individuals, as I have said. Other acts may be so small and hidden that they cannot be observed directly by another person without special equipment. Psychologists are interested in all of the acts, both large and small, as discussed in chapter 1.

Rewards

In figure 4-1, the dotted line with the arrows running from the acts back to the rewards indicates that individual acts are followed by a reward to the individual for doing the act. This reward, or possible punishment, in turn provides a new input to the person, which gives him new information to process and can thus cause him to change his responses.

The reward may be a desired event, or it may not be desired by the person. Acts followed by desired rewards tend to be repeated. In the case of undesired rewards, we frequently refer to the outcome as punishment. Punishments or the absence of desired rewards following an act reduce the tendency for the person to perform that same act the next time that input occurs. Thus, these rewards or punishments change the person in that he will now tend to process the same input differently. They may give him a new view, or a new desire, or heighten the effects of old views and desires.

Interaction of Factors

The parts of the information-processing system are not as clearly separable as the drawing in figure 4-1 would suggest. In fact, there are mutual influences among them. It is literally not possible to understand the function of any one part isolated from the rest. The total process of living and changing throughout life is dynamic and vital.

The way some psychological processes influence other psychological procedures can be illustrated by the case of selective attention. If a parent is worried about money, he may not be as interested in a project of his child or in playing with him as he would be at some other time. If he has had a rough day at the office, he may have less resistance to frustration than he would ordinarily show.

A person may have the point of view, for example, that certain desires should not be gratified because this would be ethically wrong or impractical. Because the desires call for immediate and total satisfaction, the views and desires often conflict. The decision process would attempt to work out a compromise or other solution with respect to the possible greatest rewards or smallest punishments to be expected from the various acts.

The analytic approach for understanding a person then considers his behavior to be the result of the interaction of his views, desires, and decision processes, along with limitations set by the physical apparatus. Any acts which seem irrational may be caused by the overpowering strength of unrecognized desires or views. Not only do the parts of the internal environment of the person interact complexly with one another, they also strongly affect, and are in turn affected by, the inputs and rewards. The variation of internal states means that the acts are not completely controlled by the input to the person. Sometimes the input can be so strong that it alone would control the acts. For example, if a prisoner is tortured by application of a white-hot iron to the sole of his foot, he is more likely to scream in pain than to sing an aria or to ask for a good book to read.

The student of behavior cannot be absolutely sure, however, that the branded prisoner will not make those unlikely responses. Some amazingly strong views or desires within the prisoner could impel him to perform the unlikely acts, as in the cases of martyrdom. Thus, the behavioral scientists deal in probabilities. We can only deduce what the person will probably do in a given situation. As discussed in chapter 3, we may never be able to predict human behavior with a hundred-percent accuracy.

The diagram in figure 4-1 shows a continuous cycle of behavior. As long as the person is alive, he is responding to continuous inputs with sequences of acts appropriate to his particular internal characteristics and states. The outcome (reward) following each act changes the input to the person, causing him to repeat the same act, perhaps in a more forceful fashion, or to change it. The behavior may be changed because the views or the desires of the person have changed. In such an active system, with parts constantly changing, the investigator of the causes of behavior cannot get a clear picture of any part in complete isolation from other parts. Any analytic description of the factors in figure 4-1 which determine the acts of a person must break into the cycle at some point in time which may be long after the first cause of the particular behavior started. Strictly speaking, the cause of an act that the person does today in a given situation is the sum of all the causal factors that he has previously experienced throughout his lifetime.

The preceding discussion shows the danger of concluding that the person is responding to one particular, isolated stimulus input, and not to another. The totality of inputs, past and present, must be considered in most practical life situations.

Summary

This chapter proposes the adoption of an analytic approach to the study of human behavior, the examination of individual factors which interact to produce acts. The attitude of mind which is used in understanding the functioning of, for example, an automobile, is also used in understanding the functioning of a person, because of certain items of similarity between human beings and machines.

Maturation is the emergence of the capabilities of a person to perform new acts. The stages of maturation are the same for different persons, but the timing is often different. Physical factors in the body influence both other physical factors and mental factors in various ways.

The mental processes affect both physical structures and psychological parts of a person—his views, desires, and decisions. The complex, continuing interplay of these parts of the person with the inputs and rewards of the environment ultimately produce the person's behavior.

5. Input

The environment to which a person is exposed usually influences which responses he will make. The environment may determine the immediate behavior, or it may control future behavior through developmental and learning processes. The purpose of this chapter is to describe how to produce the desired act by controlling the stimulus input.

The general idea of stimulus control is to provide one stimulus, to which the guide wants the person to respond, while eliminating other stimuli to which he might respond instead. Thus, stimulus control is an alternative to permitting the person to respond to any particular stimulus which might be present. An illustration of stimulus control from baseball is the phrase "Make him hit your pitch." The pitcher attempts to throw the ball the way the batter least likes to see it thrown. Even if the batter does hit the ball pitched this way, he is most likely to make the response desired by the pitcher—namely, a poor hit. Of course in this illustration the pitcher is not trying to guide the batter, but to control him to the pitcher's advantage.

If the person has been making a series of incorrect or nonadjustive acts, then a complete change of the stimulus input may be effective. This is what we mean when we say that a "change of scenery" may be helpful. Although the problem may not appear in the new scenery, it can however reappear when the person returns to familiar surroundings. This recurrence frequently happens in treating problems such as drug addiction or alcoholism. A temporary "cure" may be achieved in the new environment of the treatment center, but when the person returns to the same situation in which his problem appeared in the first place, he may fall once again into his previous habits. His home situation may be so depressing and intolerable that he turns to drugs, or to other measures, as a kind of psychological escape. Moreover, in the case of drugs, he is again pestered by the pusher, who is certainly trying to control his behavior, even if no one else is.

Stimulus inputs are of many kinds, and they may come from many sources. They can be internal, as from an empty stomach, or external, as from the behavior of other persons in a group. Therefore, when the guide wants to have the subject's attention, other distracting motivations should be quieted. For example, if a child is hungry in school, he may not be able to pay attention to the stimuli provided by the instructor. He may, instead, be paying attention to the insistent cries of his empty stomach. Similarly, a subject may be distracted by being cold, sick, or worried about home conditions. A worker may be distracted by such things as financial or marital problems.

This same principle of environmental control can be used to advantage, if the person tends to persist in performing undesirable acts. One way to stop him is to keep him busy with other tasks. The idea again is to avoid letting the person choose the input to which he will respond. He may be distracted from responding to the stimuli which lead to the undesired acts. Instead of saying no to the undesired acts, the guide provides stimuli to produce a different act. If the child asks for candy, which the parent does not want him to have, the parent gives him an apple, for example, or reads him a story. If the person is continuously responding to the input that the guide is providing, he will not have the time to search for other stimuli. The principle here is represented by the saying, "The devil makes work for idle hands."

If the person is producing too many acts, a general reduction of stimulation will reduce the arousal level and therefore reduce his activity. One way to do this would be to put him into a quiet room alone. This reduction of the number of possible stimuli would give him a chance to calm down. This principle is often used in school for children who tend to be overexcited. A "time-out" room permits the child to return to a more relaxed state in which he is not overresponding to the stimuli in the classroom, and thereby interfering with both his own learning and that of the other children in the class.

On the other hand, it may be important to increase the stimulation of the person. For example, if he is unmotivated or depressed, he may need more stimulation than usual. For a child, interesting toys, gadgets, designs on the wall, or tanks of fish could be beneficial. For the adult, such things as posters, books, magazines, and conversational groupings of furniture could be effective.

Getting Attention

For a stimulus to be effective in affecting the behavior of a subject, it must "get through" to him. That is, it must attract his attention at either a conscious or unconscious level. There are various techniques for drawing the attention of a person to the stimulus to which you wish him to respond. Basically these techniques increase the psychological intensity of the stimulus. For example, a speaker is more likely to get attention by speaking loudly than softly. Of course, as discussed later, the principle of contrast is important here; if he habitually shouts, he may actually get more attention by speaking in a low voice.

I think that this factor of adaptation to noise is often not understood in the education of culturally disadvantaged children. The home situation of such children is often much noisier and confused than the classroom. They are adapted to the noisy situation, and feel comfortable with a noise level that would be intolerable to the middle-class teacher. These children may have to be desensitized to the distracting quiet of the schoolroom or library before they can learn or work successfully there.

The well-known technique in advertising of associating attention-getting stimuli with the critical, message-carrying stimulus is exemplified by the use of the attractive model. Of course, in order to capture the attention of the subject, it is necessary to know something about his motivations and views. A message delivered by a hand puppet may be received by children better than the same message delivered by their parents or teachers, for example.

Another important factor in the psychological impact of a stimulus is its relative temporal position. A primacy effect means that the stimulus is favored because it appears first. Because there are not other stimuli appearing prior to it, there is no interference from some earlier response to the prior stimulation. Therefore, the first input in a situation is likely to be perceived and remembered.

The pacing of the input is also important. If too many stimuli follow in close succession, there can be an interference of the possible responses to the individual stimuli with each other. Usually, a person can do only one thing at a time, unless the tasks are very easy.

Also, as will be discussed in chapter 10, repeating an act many times in close succession will build up a tendency against making that response again, thus working against any tendency to learn it. On the other hand, a response not made for a long time is likely to be forgotten, indicating the value of a periodic review of previously learned material. Usually, it is easy to learn from his actions when the subject-person is ready to change tasks—is getting fed up with what he is doing. It nevertheless is necessary to keep in mind the need for pacing, so that you will notice the signs of boredom and distaste. Plans can be made to review the task later, in order to prevent the forgetting of the correct behaviors.

The packaging or coding of the input is also important. For example, propaganda or advertising can produce misleading cues to gain an effect. Statistics could be presented to produce an apparent background of sound scientific data. The weak data could be assimilated along with the solid evidence. Thus, the meaning of the stimulus input to the person is important. If the guide uses the language of the subject-person, inserts examples which are relevant to the person's own life, the input will have more meaning for him. Consequently, it will be more likely to be attended to and remembered, and, therefore, to influence his behavior. As will be discussed in chapter 7, the stimuli that are harmonious with the views of the observer are more often perceived and better remembered.

Another way to get the person to respond to the input is to eliminate distractors. Distractors might be toys, games, or television shows which will hold the child's attention while you are trying to get him to do his lessons. If it is not possible to eliminate distracting influences, such as those from outside noises, then the only possibility is to make sure that the person is exposed to them beforehand long enough to become adapted to them. If one is concerned with trying to establish acts in a situation that is likely to be distracting, it is important to give the individual experience with that and other different task-situations so that he will be able to make the same response in a variety of situations. He can become desensitized to the distracting stimuli. If the whole family always tiptoes when the new baby is asleep, the child may never sleep when the television is on or the family is active. If the usual family noises continue, despite the baby, the child will learn to sleep through a variety of normal noise conditions.

As mentioned above, the distractors can be used to advantage if the person is consistently making an undesirable response to some stimulus. The distractors draw his attention away from that part of the input, and direct it to a new stimulus for responding.

Total Situation

A person tends to respond to a total situation, the sum total of all input stimuli. Ordinarily, he does not respond to just one stimulus from the many that are present in his environment, but rather to that stimulus in a context of other stimuli. A simple illustration of this, taken from a study by Orbison (1939), is shown in figure 5-1. The figure in the center is in fact a square, although the lines seem to be bent because of the particular background in which they are presented. The judgment of the shape of the figure in the center of the concentric circles is influenced by the total field or background provided by the circles. Similarly, the message that one conveys to a recipient may not be just the result of the specific communications to him. It may be shaped by the entire situational atmosphere which has been created. For example, how do you convey to another person that you like him? You may tell him so, but you also back this message up by a cordial manner, a ready smile, a firm handshake, and so forth. Otherwise he might not believe the verbal message.

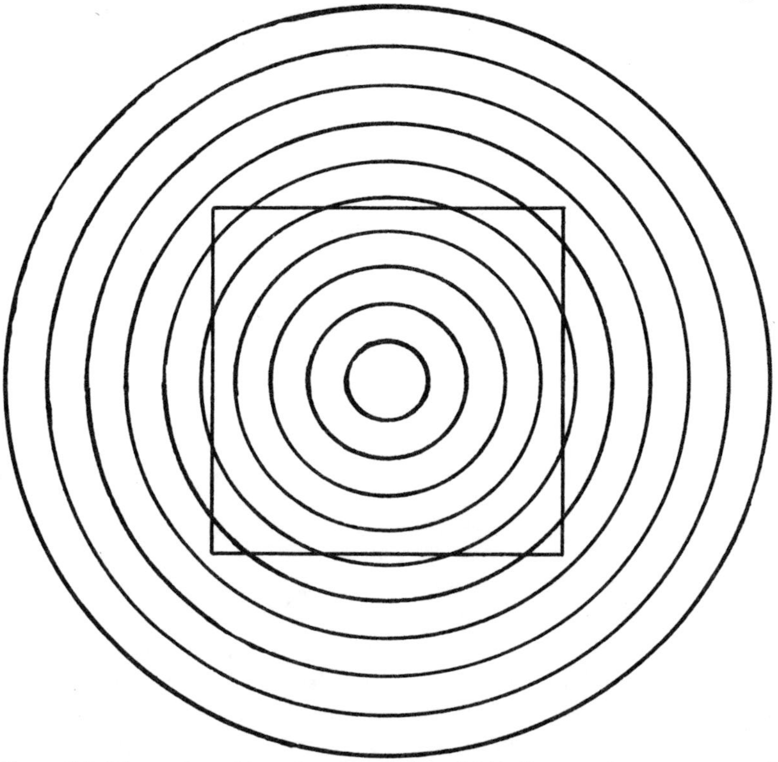

Figure 5-1. Illustration of how the surrounding field influences the appearance of a visual figure.

The response of a person is further determined by what the people around him are doing. This is frequently called the "bandwagon effect," which means that people want to be doing what others are doing—to get on the bandwagon or go along with the crowd. Children particularly imitate what they see. Putting a child in a classroom with people who are working hard should be beneficial. By the same token, putting the same child in a group that is not working, but is misbehaving, will very likely make his behavior worse. Sometimes, if a prestigious person in a group is induced to work toward the goals desired by the guide, then the others will follow.

People when in crowds often act quite differently from the way they act when alone. One illustration of this is the phenomenon of the so-called "risky shift," in which a group of people may select a course of action that is more extreme, or risky, than the response that would be predicted on the basis of their reactions as individuals. In fact, the group response may be even more extreme than that which any one person would have made by himself. Whether or not this phenomenon occurs depends upon the specific characteristics of the persons involved.

Figure 5-2. Illustration of how the meaning of the context influences the meaning of a visual figure.

The concept of the response to a total field or background is further illustrated in figure 5-2. This example is taken from a study by Bruner and Minturn (1955). If you cover the numbers 12 and 14, the figure in the center appears to be the letter "B." On the other hand, if you block out the letters "A" and "C," the figure in the center seems to be the number 13. This indicates that the meaning of the figure in the center is determined by the context provided by the surrounding stimulation. The number 13 would not fit with a series of letters, whereas the figure "B" would be inconsistent with a series of numbers. Therefore, the person perceives things to make them fit in with his other perceptions and understandings. In some circumstances, a person may even ignore an inconsistent stimulus, thinking that his perception was in error because that stimulus was not likely to have occurred. In this way we tend to ignore facts that do not fit with our prior conclusions. This fact, which is discussed in more detail in chapter 7, illustrates the close interdependence between a person's perceptions of the environment and his own personal preconceptions and biases.

On the other hand, an inconsistent stimulus may attract attention and therefore stand out in memory. One example occurred when my family and I were visiting Chinatown in San Francisco. We noticed a Virginia ham on the wall of a small grocery store. This struck us as so interesting that we actually took a picture of it. Needless to say, we probably would not have noticed a Virginia ham, much less taken a picture of it, in a store back home in Virginia. This story again emphasizes that the psychological environment of a person does not correspond exactly to his physical surroundings. Some stimuli, to which the person's attention is drawn, will seem much stronger than other stimuli to which he is not attending, even though the latter may be considerably stronger physically. In fact, when a person is concentrating his attention on one stimulus, a different one might be blocked from his awareness. My wife is familiar with this, from repeated failures to get me to answer a question when I am reading the newspaper. The "absent-minded-professor" has his attention on something other than the stimuli that others in his environment think are very obvious.

The relative nature of stimulus intensity is also illustrated by the phenomenon of adaptation. Continuous stimulation can have a decreased effect after a period of time because the person merely ceases to pay attention to it. An example of this is adapting to minor irritations. After a while the person ceases to notice the noise of a window fan, the buzzing of the fluorescent light, the pressure of the shoes on his feet. Of course, the person can become aware of this stimulation again if he has his attention called to it for some reason. I once lived across the street from a railroad track, and was at first annoyed by the noise of the trains. Later, however, I usually did not notice passing trains until someone asked me how I could stand the noise.

Psychological contrast, as well as physical contrast, can also influence perceived stimulus intensity. Contrast refers to the difference between the intensity of the stimulus and the intensity of the background stimulation to which the person is accustomed. For example, we may not notice the sound of the jet engines on the airplane because we have become adapted to their noise, but if they suddenly stop our attention is immediate, especially if we are aboard the plane. If a person has gone to sleep listening to loud music on the radio, he often wakes up when the radio is turned off.

An example of physical contrast is the fact that it is difficult to see a lighted match in an open field on a sunny day, unless you are looking directly at it. However, at night the lighted match is easily visible. In both cases the intensity of the stimulus is the same; the difference is its contrast with the background stimulation. Similarly, the teacher's voice can be heard in a quiet classroom, but not in a noisy one. The small ad is easily seen if it is all alone on the page. The absence of one worker in a shop of one hundred workers may not be noticed, but the absence of one worker in a shop of five workers would almost certainly be obvious. Therefore, the attention-getting properties of an input depend upon what other levels of stimulation are present.

The opposite of contrast is assimilation. When one stimulus is in some way different from the group in which it is included, an observer may respond to that stimulus as if it were not different from the rest, because he fails to discriminate the difference. An example of this phenomenon would be found in the old saying, "Birds of a feather flock together," or "A person is judged by the company he keeps."

Minimal Cues

Minimal cues are produced by small, perhaps weak, responses that a person may make unintentionally. These small responses nevertheless can betray more about his true attitudes and concerns than his obvious voluntary responses. These very, very small responses may communicate to other persons a completely different message from the one which the guide is consciously trying to transmit. Some people become very skilled at reading the minimal cues, when this is important. For example, a wife or husband is usually able to tell the mood of the spouse without having to be told. The caring wife has learned certain responses of the husband, of which he himself may not be aware, which tell her sometimes what he is thinking and feeling. I suspect that this ability is what some call women's intuition. The wise husband similarly studies his wife.

This reading of minimal cues is a kind of scientific mind reading, based on observing the behaviors that the mind produces and from this inferring its content. This is the observational method of science which, as mentioned in chapter 4, is used frequently in psychology.

Some people make it their business to respond to such minimal cues. For example, a friend of mine was playing poker one day when he was in the military service, and he was losing heavily. He had the unpleasant experience of having everyone else in the game drop out every time he got a good hand. It was warm and he had been playing with his shirt off. Finally, one of his friends took him aside and told him to put his shirt back on. Apparently every time he got a good hand he got excited; consequently his heart started beating faster, and its visible beating in his chest betrayed his secret.

Sports provide many illustrations of the use of minimal cues. The boxer tries to conceal the acts that he is about to do. If he inadvertently makes some small response which tells his opponent what he is about to do, he is said to be "telegraphing his punches." A baseball pitcher works very hard to make sure that nothing in his stance or delivery of the baseball betrays the kind of pitch that he is intending to throw.

Very young children learn to respond to minimal cues because they are motivated by curiosity to take in all they can about the world around them. Because the verbal cues are often not understandable to them, they must learn to interpret these other cues in order to respond correctly. Perhaps this is the reason why young children and animals can sometimes detect insincerity in a person, even when adults cannot.

Another illustration of the communication of moods or attributes by minimal cues is a story told by Dr. Carl Menninger in his book, *The Vital Balance* (1963). Menninger described an occasion when President Thomas Jefferson and some companions were riding horseback cross-country. As they prepared to cross a swollen stream, a traveler asked the President for a ride across; the President obliged him. When asked later why he had asked the President for a ride, instead of one of the other riders, the man said that some of the others had "no" on their faces, and Jefferson had a "yes" on his face. The messages conveyed by our faces through minimal cues are probably some of our most important communications to others.

Characteristics of the Guide

Obviously, the guide himself becomes a stimulus input to the subject-person, and thus his characteristics influence the subject's responses. Therefore, the guide should communicate to the subject-person the general attitude that he cares about his welfare. If the guide likes people and has respect for them as persons, he will be more effective, because his attitude will show in his behavior, through minimal cues if not the larger ones. For example, the warm and responsive schoolteacher is more effective in working with children. Unfortunately, some teachers I have known actually do not like children. They show by cues, not always minimal, that they have no respect or feeling for the pupils. The attitude of the teacher may be the most important ingredient in the motivation of the child at school.

A guide may easily, through inadvertent minimal cues, communicate his expectations to the person he intends to guide, producing what Robert Rosenthal (1966) has called a "self-fulfilling prophecy." An example of this is the superior performance of schoolchildren when the teacher expects them to do well, and also the poor work which is produced when the teacher expects them to perform poorly. We all seem to have a way of living up to, or down to, what is expected of us.

Obviously, the unconscious minimal cues will be helpful if the guide truly expects success in working toward reasonable goals; the cues will hinder his efforts if he is insincere or pessimistic. Therefore, the expectations communicated to the person should be reasonable for that person. For example, if one is dealing with retarded children, the expectations should be pitched to their level. Similarly, one would expect more from the gifted child.

A successful guide avoids the "hard sell." The application of pressure or the arousal of fear is not effective in producing a rational adjustive response, because excessively strong emotion interferes with learning. Even if there is learning, this process is not conducive to the development of mental health. We can arouse fear and show how our proposals will reduce the fear. It may work. But it can also boomerang. The person may become angry that his guide has aroused his fear, and then he will resist further guidance.

Individual differences are important here, as always, because different people react differently to authoritarian treatment. Some people resist and do exactly the opposite of what the authoritarian suggests; others tend to knuckle under and do exactly what he orders. In general, however, autocratic handling of workers causes production to go down and stay down, because it tends to lower a person's self-esteem, making him lower his expectations for himself and causing emotional stress and unhappiness, which in turn impair his capacity to learn. To function at his best, a person should be consulted before a policy is formulated, not handed a course of action toward some goal and told to follow it.

The guide who is genuinely interested in his subject-person will try to increase his own effectiveness by improving his image with the subject. For example, the guide who is perceived by the subject as expert and trustworthy is more likely to influence that person than one seen as clumsy or hypocritical.

Duration of Stimulation

In attempting to control a person by controlling his environment, the length of time he spends in the environment is obviously important. Therefore, schoolteachers may work with parents, fellow teachers, and superintendents to establish broader control of the environment of the child. Unfortunately for many children, such cooperation does not always take place, and they are in a good school environment for only a small fraction of each day, for only some days.

This problem of lack of cooperation has the worst effects on the very children who would benefit most from a good school environment. Some parents of the culturally disadvantaged child do not appreciate the need for school attendance. One child in a special education program typically was absent from thirty-five to forty times each school year, for trivial excuses. Most often he was absent just because he did not want to go to school, and his parents did not consider it important to make him go.

Persistence of Stimulation

Effects of stimulation can persist in the central nervous system after the external stimulus has ceased, for many days in the case of the human being. If a person has been insulted or frustrated, for example, the effects may persist for a very long time. Moreover, the resulting high level of continuing arousal may add to some later input to produce an exaggerated response. If the person is already aroused because of some prior input, he may overreact to an innocuous input that normally would not excite him. For example, if the day has been generally quiet and peaceful, a person may be quite able to take some petty annoyance in his stride—such as listening to the person at the next desk crack his knuckles, or waiting in the long line at the traffic light. This same "petty" annoyance can be "the last straw" and cause one to "blow his top" if earlier in the day he has experienced a series of similar annoyances or a major reprimand by the boss.

On the other hand, the person could underreact to an input. He may be so upset and concerned about a previous frustration, for example, that he loses his appetite and refuses to eat even a most desired food. For the moment, the sight and smell of apple pie may not be strong enough to "take his mind off," to distract him from, his problems. He may be so depressed and generally "down" from some previous defeat that he may have lost his will to fight some new source of frustration. Therefore, when a person makes a response that is quite different from his usual, expected reaction to a given situation, we can judge that he is troubled or distracted in some way.

Generalization

An important problem in controlling stimulus situations, as a way of controlling responses, is to know to what extent acts will be transferred from one situation to another. Often the guide desires to transfer a response from one situation to a different one. For example, the parent teaches table etiquette at home so that the child will exhibit good manners when he is at a friend's home. To promote the transfer, the parent tries to show ways in which the two different situations—parent's home and friend's home—are in fact similar to one another, requiring the same responses.

You would hope that the kind thoughts and gentle behavior generated in church on the Sabbath would be generalized to many different situations at other times during the week. An illustration of this was made most strikingly some years ago by a college student who showed up at a church meeting wearing cut-off pajamas. His explanation was that these were his "study clothes," usually worn in his room at the college, and that we should not make clearcut distinctions between our "religious" lives and our "secular" lives.

Good responses should be transferred or generalized to many new environments and situations. Thus, it is important to make the home, classroom, or other situations in which he is to respond, pleasant for the subject. The attitudes developed in the one situation can transfer to the material being learned in a similar situation.

A person responds not only to the press of the existing environment, but also to his perception of future events. These predictions of the future depend upon his interpretation of the present surroundings and upon his past experience with similar ones. This certainly adds to the difficulty of predicting what response he will make.

Discrimination

There are times when the guide does not want acts to transfer from one situation to another. Then he tries to help his subject-person make discriminations among situations so that the person can respond appropriately to different ones. For example, the proper acts in the cheering section of a football stadium on a weekday would be quite different from those expected in church on the Sabbath. By the same token, we would not want the football player to transfer his aggressive acts from the football field on Saturday afternoon to the social affair on Saturday evening. We hope that the soldier confines his killing to the enemy troops, if he believes that he must kill, without extending this response to include civilians.

Similarly, we do not discourage all anger, but anger that does not allow the proper discriminations to be made. We should become angry at slum lords, child beaters, rapists, and the like, where the anger leads us toward productive behaviors for solving problems.

There are, however, limits on our ability to discriminate among stimuli, some of which are set by our physical structure. For example, the human eye is not able to detect radio waves or ultraviolet light, and therefore these stimuli can have little direct effect on our behavior.

As one becomes older or more mature, he is able to make more discriminations than before, just as he is also able to generalize more. The important aim is to be able to recognize the readiness of a child to make certain discriminations. If we ask a child or handicapped person to make a discrimination which is beyond his capability, he will, of course, become frustrated. If a child is too young to discriminate between situations, he cannot be expected to respond differently to them.

A child with special problems, such as a hearing or visual deficit, often develops behavioral problems when his handicap is not recognized. Sometimes such a child is judged to be mentally retarded because he does not make the responses which the normal child would give. If a person cannot learn to make discriminations, his ability to discriminate may be at fault, rather than his ability to learn. A problem arises if the parents do not realize that the child fails to respond correctly only when sight or hearing are required, for example.

A clear differentiation between the situation in which the person is expected to perform the desired act and the situation in which he will be allowed to rest or relax is helpful. For example, a student should have a time and a place for studying; he should avoid doing other things in that place in the presence of those stimuli. For example, it is not wise to play tiddlywinks on our study desk, or sleep in our study chair, because the urge to play tiddlywinks or sleep may thereafter become too strong whenever we sit down to study.

We can learn to discriminate among different stimuli, or to improve our ability to discriminate. The importance of the correct perception of stimuli is indicated by the old story of the person who received a fat lip when he thought that a rugged bruiser said, "Stand up," when he had in fact said, "Shut up." A discrimination between two stimuli or stimulus situations is achieved by providing different conditions of reward for the acts in each situation; this subject will be discussed further in chapter 10. A reward is given to the person when he performs the correct or appropriate act in response to the correct or appropriate input. He may even be punished for responding to the wrong input.

Summary

This chapter discusses how controlling the immediate environment of a person can influence his acts. The goal of such an approach is to provide the person with strong stimuli which evoke the desired response, and to eliminate the stimuli which lead to nonadjustive, competing acts. Various methods for drawing a person's attention to the stimuli to which he should respond include control of physical attributes of the stimulus, such as intensity and frequency of presentation, and use of other principles, such as contrast and the elimination of distractors.

The importance of the attitude of the guide, as interpreted through "minimal cues," was also analyzed. These cues, produced by tiny acts of the guide or by other factors in the situation, communicate a climate of feeling which tells the subject-person whether or not he is highly esteemed. Such cues also communicate expectations to the person which are likely to influence his behavior. Because a person typically responds to a total situation, rather than to some specific stimulus, the context in which a stimulus input is placed is important. The acts of other people in his environment tend to induce imitative behavior and to facilitate performance of similar acts.

Generalization and discrimination processes were described and discussed. Generalization means a carry-over, or transfer, of learned acts—producing an act learned in response to one stimulus or in one situation in response to a different stimulus or in a different situation. Discrimination means restricting acts to narrower ranges of appropriate situations. Decisions about the proper range of situations in which to deliver a given act depend upon the particulars of the input conditions and upon the desired acts.

6. Personal Desires

Everyone needs and wants something. The key to understanding and guiding the actions of another is to understand his motivation, to discover what he desires enough to work for. If you have some control over whether or not the person gets what he wants, then you have the means to change his behavior.

Consider the familiar saying: "You can lead a horse to water, but you cannot make him drink." Although this is true in one sense, in another very real sense it is not. Any direct attempt to force the horse to drink will of course upset the horse, and actually decrease the probability that he will drink. An indirect approach will work, however. Because the horse will drink when he is thirsty, your method is merely to make him thirsty.

In the same way, the child can be led to perform desirable acts if you discover which conditions give him the proper motivation. Even though he may not want to eat his spinach, he will do so gladly when he becomes sufficiently hungry. The guide has to have sufficient determination to withhold other food until the child gets hungry enough to eat the spinach. Whether or not the parent goes through this procedure, and puts the child through it, is determined by how important the parent considers spinach to be for the diet of the child. Is it really necessary to change this particular behavior? Perhaps some other leafy green vegetable would do as well.

There is little change in behavior when there is little motivation for the person to change. Thus, the importance of motivation in learning new acts cannot be overemphasized. John Dewey (1946) built his approach to education on this notion. He argued that, because proper "school behavior" is not the result of natural desires of young children, the teacher must find out which motivations the child *does* have and build upon them for effective learning in the school situation. For example, the child might not care to study mathematics, but he might want to learn some mathematical rules which would be helpful to him in laying out a baseball diamond.

The primary problem of the guide, then, is to discover what desires the person has; then he can use this knowledge for motivating the proper behavior. Unfortunately, some people who should know better do not understand this principle. A very experienced schoolteacher was one. In discussing the progress of a child who did not achieve the success in school that would be expected on the basis of his ability—he was a so-called underachiever—she pointed out that he did not try hard enough. This was hardly a surprising insight, to be sure! She further remarked that she had no patience with a child who had ability, but who would not work; she would not waste time trying to teach such a child. This experienced, but ignorant, teacher was thereby failing in the most important job of a guide—to motivate the person to learn, to want to change his behavior.

If the person wants to learn, the job of teaching is easy, of course. It is merely a matter of making information available. For the mature student, as is found in postgraduate or professional schools, the professor can correctly assume that at least most of his students are eager to learn. At the other developmental extreme, the very young preschool child also probably wants very much to learn, because he is still curious about things. Unfortunately, the child who has been exposed to school seems to be the one who lacks the motivation to learn the school subjects, probably because too many of us, like the teacher described above, have not appreciated the necessity for supporting the motivation of those whom we hope to guide. If we expect everyone, student or worker, child or adult, to be a "self-starter," we are not taking individual differences into account properly. For some persons, the motivation to perform the correct actions must be stimulated—or even created.

Individual persons have different collections of desires, of course. The different desires in all probability have different strengths, with the relative strengths probably varying in different situations and at different times. Someone may prefer to eat popcorn at the movies, but peanuts at the circus. John may prefer to take Mabel to the ball game, but Matilda to the opera. This is another illustration of interactions among causal factors.

Some stimulus inputs such as pain are ordinarily not desired by anyone. Thus, the person will typically perform an act to escape from pain if he can. If he does not, we look for some reason that the experiences of the person have caused him to desire the pain more than he desires the absence of pain. This idea is expressed when we say, sometimes seriously and sometimes not, "I would rather be beaten than do this." As a child I often developed a headache when it was my turn to wash the dishes. The spouse who says, "Not tonight, honey, I have a headache," may actually have one. What caused it is the question. What is the gain from the pain?

Some of the desires of a person may be in conflict with one another in a given situation. A factory worker probably has the desire to be safe in his work, and he probably also has the desire to make as much money as he can. One man made a safety device on a stamping machine inoperative in order to speed up his production, and thereby earn more incentive pay. The machine would not operate until two buttons were pressed simultaneously—one with each hand—thereby keeping the operator's hands out of the machine. The worker placed a brick over one button to keep it depressed, allowing him to feed material into the machine with one hand, operating it with the other. Therefore, to increase his income, he deliberately risked the undesired outcome of having his hand crushed.

Another illustration of the principle that one must understand a person's desires in order to understand his behavior comes from an experiment at a large university. A visitor to the laboratory observed a rat in a box grasping an electrified knob, which was delivering a noxious electric shock to him. The rat merely had to let go of the knob to avoid the shock. Thus, his behavior seemed to be quite stupid, in defiance of the laws governing the motivation of behavior. This behavior did however make sense when one learned that the rat had been trained to grasp the knob in order to turn off a more severe shock to his feet through a grid on the floor. Once the rat had learned to hold the knob, the sly experimenter had turned off the shocking device on the floor. Whereas the rat's response had initially been quite adaptive and sensible, later it failed to serve the original purpose. It was still serving a purpose, but now a new one. The rat was choosing a response which was painful to him, but less painful than what he perceived to be the alternative. Our added knowledge about the experience of the rat indicates that his behavior was not truly stupid but caused by very appropriate motivation, to decrease his fear of the shock from the floor grid. Similarly, even though a person does something without apparent cause that seems to be stupid or unreasonable, it will probably not seem so if the history, desires, and life situation of that individual become known. Thus, some desires are learned and are consequently not predictable unless one knows something about the personal history of the individual. Chapter 10 discusses how these desires are learned, and why they persist.

Unfortunately, human beings, like the rat in the above story, often cling to old habits that were once effective, but that now are not helpful, and are possibly harmful, to them. Apparently the individual continues to receive some reward for making these old responses, even though the old response does not produce the original gain. So long as the rat in the above story clings to the electrified knob, he does not have to fear the strong shock from the floor grid. But at the same time, he cannot learn that the floor shock will not come, and that there is nothing to fear from it. If he does not test reality—if he never checks to find out whether or not the floor shock will come when he fails to grab the knob—then he will continue to receive the needless jolts from the knob.

An example of the same type of situation in human relations would be the case of the worker who volunteers to take the initiative on some project. As a result, he is criticized, or the project fails. He may avoid such criticism and failure experiences in the future by refusing ever again to take any initiative beyond required tasks. This might stand in his way for raises or promotions, if the company truly wants to see such initiative by their personnel. The earlier unfortunate experience might have been unusual, because a boss had a bad day, or some other such temporary circumstances affected the result. Or it may be that there is now a new boss, a new company policy, and so forth. In any case, the motivation learned earlier to avoid taking initiative might now be harmful to the person, so that new motivation is needed. The worker, like the rat in the earlier example, might continue to pay the price of a lack of initiative if he fails to test current reality.

To be sure, such a test would reasonably be set up to minimize the pain if the situation were still unchanged. The smart rat would stand on his toes near the safety knob. The worker would make some tentative, "feeler" responses of initiative, and observe the reactions. It is not necessary to dive into a lake to discover whether or not the water is warm enough for swimming; simple immersion of a tip of a toe provides enough information.

Because all behavior is caused by existing input, desires, or views, there is a reason for every act, even though this cause may not be obvious at first glance. The person himself may not however be aware of his own motivation. If the behavior seems to be unreasonable and against the best interests of the person, then the discovery of the desires which are responsible for it may be very difficult or impossible. For example, a teenager may turn down the opportunity to go out to dinner with the family, which ordinarily is a highly desired event. The parents may never learn that he is expecting an important telephone call and does not want anyone to know how important it is to him. So, he mystifies the parents by giving some obviously inappropriate excuse—like he is afraid of getting sunburned riding in the car, or he has to study for a test next month.

If the resulting acts are not very important, such as the choice of a particular brand of breakfast cereal on a given morning, we do not concern ourselves about them. We merely explain them as the result of trivial personal preferences—unless we happen to manufacture breakfast cereals, of course. If the acts are important, such as persistent tendencies of the person to enjoy torturing animals, we take a more serious view, because such desires are sufficiently out of line with ordinary motivations that some professional help in straightening them out is probably required.

The question of whether or not therapeutic intervention to cure the person with a problem is advisable depends upon how incapacitated the person is by his unnecessary fear or unusual desire. It is also influenced by psychological, physical, and financial cost of the therapy to the individual, and by the potential risks to others.

Readiness and Change

Desires change as a result of the maturation of the physical apparatus and through experience. The guide should be prepared for these changes as they occur. When my son was very young, he followed me around like most sons, trying to do the things that I did. He even had his own little toy lawn mower, imitating me as I mowed the lawn. As he has grown, he has become a greater help in doing the various jobs about the house, such as mowing the grass—much to my pleasure. Although I ordinarily enjoy seeing my son grow and develop, I naturally had mixed emotions, however, when he made an insightful remark one day while inspecting the lawn that needed mowing. "You know, Dad," he said, "I decided that the jobs you wanted to do as a kid, you don't want to do when you get old enough."

Stages

The newborn child is governed by purely selfish desires, merely wanting his physical needs satisfied. Later he learns that he depends upon others to satisfy his needs. Therefore, as he matures, he develops desires to please other people also, because this is to his advantage.

The sequences of the various stages of development are predictably the same for various children, although the rates of progress are often different, as was discussed previously. Therefore, it is easier to know what stage a child is in and what stage will be entered next than it is to know when the change to the next stage will occur.

To understand and to be prepared for the various stages of maturation helps a parent to live through them. When my son was going through the stage of competing with father and finding fault with just about everything I tried to do, I understood that this was a normal part of the development of the proper sex role. Although I understood it, it was still rather hard on old dad. When I complained about it to a family friend, hoping for sympathy, her response made me feel much better. She said, "Well, you wouldn't want it the other way, would you?" Indeed, I was glad to see signs of the development of the proper sex role.

Maturation vs. Motivation

Although a person may be perfectly able to make a response, he may not have the desire to make it. Therefore, if a person does not perform some act, it does not mean that he in fact cannot. For example, a child may not speak if he has no need to talk. If the parents are good enough at anticipating his wants, he does not have to ask for anything. Consequently, a very intelligent child might not talk until long after the normal age of saying first words—obviously producing great concern on the part of the parents.

Other motivational or emotional factors can block performance of a response that the child is capable of making. A true story illustrates this. My son had begun speaking a word or two at the age of about one year, at which time I changed jobs and moved to another city. The excitement and general confusion of moving caused him to stop speaking entirely. Not only was there no evidence of any language development, for a time he did not speak at all. He was still learning, however, as was proved later. His next word was included in a complete sentence, drawn out by motivation which has proven to be characteristic of him. He said, "I want a cookie."

How to Discover Motivations

Several procedures help us to discover a person's desires. For example, some desires are expected of all persons because they are human beings. Because they have about the same physical apparatus, they generally have the same physical desires. They need food and drink in order to survive, for example. These desires are not dependent upon the person having particular life experiences.

Examining Experiences

Other desires are learned. Therefore, some knowledge of the person's particular experiences is required in order to discover these particular desires. For example, a man who is very interested in athletics and who frequently takes his son to athletic events is very likely to produce a son who enjoys athletics. Whatever motivation has been consistently rewarded in the past, because the responses which it produced were rewarded, will be a probable motivation in the future.

Verbal Questioning

Another way to find out what a person wants is to ask him. What he says is not necessarily true, however, because he may lie. Also, people do not always know what their true desires are and therefore cannot always report them accurately. This was illustrated at a meeting at our church, called for the purpose of establishing greater communication between adults and youth. Although the sheer fact of the meeting helped for this purpose, the adults afterward still did not appear to have a good grasp of what the young people wanted. A primary reason for this was given by the comment of one youth, who said, "We don't know what we want." Other comments did indicate that, although they did not know what specific desires to formulate, they did want to feel like persons of worth, whose presence and support was valued by the rest of the congregation.

Obviously, too, a person does not always want what he asks for. This would be particularly true for young children or for adults with insufficient self-understanding. The child often tests to find any exceptions to the rules laid down by the parents; he may just want to reassure himself that they still provide firm anchors of security in a changing, confusing world. Teenagers may ask for certain privileges because they will lose face with their friends if they do not ask for them. Workers may present the foreman with impossible demands, in order to determine whether or not he will be a strong leader.

The immature person may want something briefly and then quickly shift his desires to something entirely different. This is valuable to keep in mind when the young child mentions what he wants to be when he grows up. His goal may change many times before he is mature enough to select a realistic goal.

Observing Acts

Often we can tell more accurately what a person desires by the acts he performs than by what he says. A young man may claim that he desires the company of Mary more than that of Jane, but if he asks Jane for more dates, we question either his self-understanding or his honesty. A person may claim to like good literature, but if he reads only comic books we again doubt that he has told the truth. A person may claim to want to be thin, but if he eats instead of dieting we conclude that he has another, stronger motivation. Another person may claim to have strong desires to help other people, but if he only performs services for which he is paid or which otherwise benefit him, we doubt his claim. All of this is summarized by the old saying, "Actions speak louder than words."

Because spoken words are also actions, the above saying requires a little interpretation. The idea is to use judgment about the weight put on the different actions. As another saying goes, "Talk is cheap," meaning that a person ordinarily does not have to work as hard to produce words as he does to perform other acts. This is not true for all people, of course; some persons may find it easier to show in other actions what they cannot put into words.

Thus, all actions should be examined before one reaches a conclusion about the motivation. In the above-mentioned case of the boy asking for dates, he may be too fearful of asking Mary for dates, even though he likes her better than Jane. We might reach the correct conclusion if we notice that the youth tends to stammer and blush in Mary's presence, but not in Jane's. He may remember Mary's birthday and keep track of where she is at all times. If he fails to do this with Jane, we have additional clues to the truth.

The best indication of what desires a person will have is knowledge of what he has desired under similar circumstances in the past. This consistency of desires and acts leads us to classify people into what is called personality types. We might say that the person is an introvert—meaning that he tends to avoid social contact. Or we may say that he is an extrovert—meaning that he apparently enjoys meeting other people socially. Such typing of people may help as a first approximation, but one must remember that psychological types are not clearcut. For example, the extreme cases of either extroversion or introversion are rare. The hermit, who always wants to be alone regardless of the circumstances, is the exception. So too is the person who must always be in the crowd. Most of us are some combination of the two; we sometimes like to be around people, and at other times we want to be alone. Whether or not we want to mix with others is controlled by many specific factors—how long it is since we have been by ourselves, our particular mood, how well we like and get along with the other person, and so forth.

Other psychological types might be dominant vs. submissive, or masculine vs. feminine, and the like. Again, the difficulty with such typing is that it lends itself to stereotyped thinking. That is, a person is placed into a type on the basis of certain of his actions, and is then considered to have all of the characteristic attributes of that type, whether or not this is true. Even a classification like masculinity or femininity shows that most persons have some attributes, or traits, that are characteristic of the other type. That is, most men have a few so-called feminine traits and most women have a few so-called masculine traits. Therefore, even within a "type," there is ample room for broad individual variations.

Creating the Motivation

Desires can be stimulated or created. For example, under some conditions, the guide might find it necessary to use bribes or threats. The parent might bribe a child to study for an hour with the promise of an ice cream cone. In this case the deal is made in advance. Alternatively, the parent may threaten the child with some punishment if he fails to study. Although bribery is better than threats, neither procedure is as effective as using the natural desires of the person. As will be discussed in chapter 10, the guide is more likely to succeed if he allows the person to make the proper act on his own, and then satisfies his desire for something. The guide obviously has a difficult problem if the person would never produce the correct act on his own. Then the guide is forced to rearrange the conditions in some way in order to increase the chances that the subject-person will perform a correct or nearly correct action, or to "shape" the behavior, as discussed in chapter 10.

If the person does not have the desire to perform an act that you want him to perform, you may have to create such a desire. This is obviously important for salespersons, for example. The act that the seller wants to see is, of course, purchase of his wares. When I was a salesman in a clothing store during my college days, my boss had a favorite rule: "If you don't have what they want, make them want what you have." Because the salesperson usually has no personal knowledge of the customer, he must rely on the generality of human desires. For example, he can assume that the prospective customer has the usual desire to conform and says, "All of the college students are wearing them this year" or "I sold one of these to the mayor last week." Or he can take a chance on the person's specific motivation, and say, "These are designed to make you look slimmer." As my boss used to say, the ability to satisfy the needs of the customer is the difference between a salesperson and a package-wrapper.

Physical Causes

Physically based motivations are familiar to us because everyone has them. They include immediate needs, which must be satisfied in a relatively short period of time if the person is to survive, and long-term needs, which are not concerned with immediate survival but may be necessary eventually.

Immediate Needs

Probably the most familiar examples of immediate needs are for food and water. If a person refuses to eat or drink, we seek causes, of which there are many. It may be that he has just finished dinner, or maybe he is too shy to eat in front of strangers. He may even be on a hunger strike. He may eat only kosher food, and you have offered him nonkosher food. He may be sick or have an injury to his brain that prevents him from eating.

Other desires are related to the need for air and to the need to eliminate wastes from the body. These require no further discussion since they are universally familiar.

Long-Term Needs

The desire for sleep is of course also familiar. Although this need does not require satisfaction as quickly as the need for air, it can become very demanding eventually. Lack of sleep can make one aroused and irritable, and it can interact with other sources of arousal.

The need for sex, too, is based on our physical structure. It is more obviously present in the sexually mature person. Although some persons survive without sexual gratification, there is abundant reason to believe that most people do not prefer this.

Other long-term needs are not quite so obvious to us, but they are nevertheless important. Examples of these are curiosity and the need for muscle activity. Although some psychologists have doubted that these desires are based on physical structure alone, it is a safe bet that they are present, in any case. These desires are of course molded somewhat by a person's experience. For example, he is curious about and is led to explore situations that are unfamiliar to him. Once he has gained sufficient experience with a situation, it tends to bore him. As the child satisfies his curiosity, he is gaining experience with different situations that prepare him for later adjustments to life.

A child cooped up at home on a rainy Saturday will want to move about vigorously by the end of the day. The same is true for that child confined to his schoolroom. Adults have the same problems. They will want to "stretch their legs" after a long automobile trip or after a long tenure on the production line. Adults are not as "fidgety" because they have learned to keep their desires under better control; also, they are not asked to stay confined to a chair for long periods as are school children.

Just as the person will eventually get bored with a stimulus situation, he will also become bored with an extended activity. No matter how much a person likes an activity, if he repeats it over and over again without sufficient pauses for rest he will cease to desire it. It might even become aversive. He must rest, "take a break," before he wants to pursue that activity again. We are familiar with the child who plays with a Christmas toy continuously for hours and then loses interest in it. This is the danger of letting, or making, a person perform any activity for too long. He may build up such an aversion to it that he never performs that act voluntarily again. If the activity is beneficial, like practicing the piano or homework, then too much drill on it will be harmful. Some of my schoolteachers never understood that principle!

By the same reasoning, if an activity is harmful, then forced repetition of it may help to eliminate it. The determination of how much practice is beneficial to a desired skill and of how much will actually hinder its development requires judgment by the person guiding the behavior.

The interesting thing about the curiosity and the activity motivations is that they are satisfied by an increase in input to the brain from the sense organs, rather than by a decrease in stimulation. In general, the satisfaction of physical desires, like hunger, requires a shutting off or reduction of input to the brain. For example, the stomach no longer is telling the brain that it is empty; the bowels stop sending messages that something must be done after it has occurred. The stimulus-seeking motivations, on the other hand, represent an attempt of the person to keep his level of internal arousal within desired limits by increasing, instead of decreasing, the level of arousal. The limits of desired arousal levels would presumably be different for different types of motivations. The person may not want to tolerate very much arousal from an empty stomach, but he might increase the sensory experience of ingesting food by adding spicy sauces.

Even the motivations to reduce input are frequently increased briefly just before satisfaction in order to increase the pleasure of the satisfaction. For example, a person will have an appetizer before dinner. The young child may hold his bowel movement as long as he can because it feels so good when he finally lets go. Perhaps the best example of the deliberate increase in stimulation before a satisfactory decrease is the use of foreplay in sexual behavior. The participants strive for mutual arousal up to the point of final satisfaction in order to improve the pleasure which it provides.

The preferred levels of arousal would also be different for different people, of course. Some people like massive amounts of external stimulation and thus take up skydiving or big-game hunting with bow and arrow. Others are more easily satisfied, content with riding roller-coasters or ferris wheels. Still others get all of the activation they want by watching soap operas on television.

Learned Causes

Although the presence of physically caused desires does not depend upon experience, the particular way of satisfying them may be affected by experience. For example, some people satisfy hunger by eating snails and chocolate-covered ants, while some like yogurt and cottage cheese and others favor meat and potatoes. While all of these items can satisfy the need for food, their desirability varies from person to person. Psychologists use the concept of "incentive" to refer to this learned degree of preference for some satisfiers over others. Other desires may be completely the result of learning. As mentioned above, there is frequent disagreement among psychologists about whether certain desires are learned or innate.

Incentives

Incentives refer to objects or conditions that a person perceives as capable of satisfying his desires. Consequently, the person will be likely to perform some act to which an incentive is attached. The incentive is the carrot suspended on the stick before the donkey to cause him to run forward. Perhaps the most familiar use of the term is in the expression "incentive pay." This is the practice of determining a rate of pay for a person by the amount that he accomplishes—frequently called the piece rate. The person is paid by the number of gears that he makes, or the number of baskets of beans picked, or the number of telephones assembled. Presumably, the person who is more skilled and who works harder will earn more of the incentive pay.

The desirability of incentives is determined by the past experience of the person as well as by his immediate desires and the prevailing conditions. The ice cream cone is only an incentive if the person is hungry and likes ice cream. Gold has little value as an incentive for a person dying of thirst in the middle of the desert. Money is likely to be more of an incentive to a poor boy than a rich one; fame and prestige would probably be stronger incentives for the boy who has been born rich.

Experience can act in an opposite way. Although a woman whose mother had been a poor housekeeper would probably turn out to be a poor housekeeper also, she might on the other hand become excessively scrupulous in her approach to this task, with a spotless house as her incentive. If the latter case occurred, we would say that this person overreacted to her earlier experience. Another example of this would be parents who have themselves been reared by excessively restrictive and controlling parents and who then become overly permissive with their own children, setting no limits at all on what they do. In their effort to avoid the mistake of their parents, they make the opposite one.

If a person has not had the same experiences as another, it is difficult for him to anticipate all of the things that are incentives for the other person. This fact was brought clearly to my mind while listening to a lecture on the educational problems of inner-city black children. The speaker described the greater importance of having the schools open earlier in the morning than in a middle-class neighborhood, because the children tended to arrive long before classes began. Because their homes were often unheated, they wanted to be where it was warm. Particularly, they wanted to be able to use a warm bathroom.

Similarly, we assume that our own incentives have the same values for others. A number of years ago I had the distressing experience of having a cultured neighbor mention to me, very hesitantly, that my garbage can smelled, and that she would appreciate it if I would scrub it out. She was, unfortunately, quite justified in her complaint, much to my embarrassment. I complied with her request, and resolved never again to be placed in such an unpleasant situation. Imagine my shock when I came home one evening some weeks later and was met by a very unpleasant odor. I told my wife that I must rush out quickly to apologize to the lady and take care of the garbage can again. She stopped me in time; the good lady was cooking sweetbreads for her supper.

The history of a possible incentive is important. If a child were given nothing but ice cream for several days, eventually he would probably refuse to eat any more even if he were mildly hungry and would eat other things. If a waitress is accustomed to dollar tips, a fifty-cent tip is not much of an incentive for her to provide good service. On the other hand, if the usual tip is ten cents, fifty cents is a good incentive. If one nation has been getting $10 million in foreign aid from another government for many years, it becomes furious if the amount is cut to only $5 million in a particular year. Therefore, if the person does not expect much, he will be happy with what he gets. If he expects a large incentive, he will not be pleased with a moderate amount. If he expects unreasonable amounts, he will probably never be pleased. This principle will be fully discussed in chapter 8.

The value of an object as an incentive is also related to how hard one has to work for it. If the person has to work hard for an item, he values it more. The parent may value an object highly, because he worked a long time for it, but his child may take it for granted. The easily available item tends to be treated with contempt. The precious gem is valued precisely because it is rare.

In listing the various incentives in the order of their effectiveness in satisfying desires, we should not assume that money is at the top of the list. The old saying, "Money isn't everything, but it is way ahead of what is second," is not true. As Gagné and Fleishman (1959) conclude in their book on human performance in industry, money is involved in the satisfaction of both physical needs, like hunger, and learned needs, such as personal status, but the studies which have been made on what workers want almost never show money as being first on the list. These writers go on to say, however, that pay was always on the list of things desired. Obviously, the amount of pay would be most important for a person who was barely making enough money to satisfy his physical needs. For persons at a higher level, the personal meaning of the salary becomes important. For example, the relative amounts of pay that two workers receive is a tangible indication of how much the employers value each man. A college professor once said that he was not really concerned about the amount of his pay, but merely that he be paid as much as his institution could afford to pay him. The indication that he was wanted and valued by the institution maintained his self-esteem; this was more important than the exact amount of money he could put in his pocket.

The arousal of fear is not effective as an incentive for producing a favorable, reasoned response. In the first place, high emotions tend to interfere with learning, as will be discussed later in this chapter. Although the guide might arouse fear and show how the acts which he recommends will reduce the fear, this can produce a backlash if the person becomes angry that his fear has been aroused. Also, the person can learn to avoid all contact and communications with the guide if the guide arouses unpleasant feelings.

Psychological Needs

All of the desires to be discussed in this section may not be completely the result of learning. It is beyond the scope of this book to consider whether or not only experience is involved in producing certain desires. Such a question is difficult to answer because in certain respects all animals of a given species do have similar experiences. The acts which result from such experiences are therefore found in all members of the species. Because the appearance of a given act in all members of the species provides one indication that it is the result of the common physical structure, the learned desire could be mistaken for a physically-based one. In any case, learning is important in directing and shaping these desires.

The importance of self-esteem in connection with money was mentioned in the preceding section. Possibly all of the individual psychological needs are just specific manifestations of this basic need. Examples of specific psychological needs are the need to achieve, to compete, and to conform. These all seem to be bound up with the person's desire to be approved of by others and to approve of himself. How he does this is determined to a great extent by what society expects and supports. In particular, ways to gain approval and acceptance are determined by the ideas and attitudes of the members of a person's own group whom he sees as equal to him in social status, ability, and in other important aspects.

A person competes in different ways, depending upon what his society prefers. American society is known for its competitiveness in the accumulation of material wealth. The idea is to "win all of the marbles." In some societies, however, the object is to be the best "*non*-competer" or "*non*-achiever," as in the game of give-away checkers, in which the goal is to make your opponent jump more of your men than you jump of his. The winner is the first person to *lose* all of his checkers. Another example is the practice of awarding a prize for being the worst-dressed person at the masquerade ball.

An example of psychological needs expressed in terms of conformity and non-conformity was once familiar in our society. The so-called hippies apparently did strive to create highly personalized costumes, which were deliberately designed not to conform to the clothing of the members of the larger society—the establishment. In so doing, they developed dress and manners which marked them as members of an easily identified group, wearing the hippie "uniform." In rejecting one set of standards for conformity, they adopted and conformed to a different set of standards. In failing to conform to the standards of the "bathed," they conformed to the standards of the "not bathed."

Obviously, the standards set by a particular group may change over time. What was usual behavior in past years is often not acceptable today. Often the acts which were rewarded during the youth of a person are not at all appreciated as he grows older. But the acts, and views which were responsible for them, may be held on to long after their value has gone. This contributes to what we have come to call the generation gap. Modern parents of college students lived through the Great Depression and World War II, and, therefore, were accustomed to shortages of just about everything. Modern youth, on the other hand, have known mostly relative plenty, although to be sure not all of them have shared in the good times. The youth in turn have a clearer interest in preserving the environment because they can reasonably expect more years during which to enjoy it, or to have to endure it.

The demands of conformity can be stronger than other motivations, of course. For example, children will often deny a desire because they think that it will cause them to lose face in the eyes of their friends. They do not want to do certain desired acts in a way that would seem voluntary to their friends. If they are "made" to do them, then they have a good excuse if they are caught. The other day a parent described his child as the type that would say to himself, "I'm going to be late for school today if someone doesn't pretty soon tell me to hurry."

The desire to imitate others is ordinary in our society. The child perhaps first learns to imitate the mother. Later, he learns to imitate his like-sexed parent. He is rewarded for this; everyone thinks that it is cute for the boy to behave just like Daddy. Later, he may switch to select Babe Ruth or Fidel Castro as his model, or he may select some member of his own group who is held in high esteem.

Probably because of self-esteem, people desire to set goals for themselves. When they do this, the motivation to do the job is guaranteed. If a person has selected his goals on the basis of his existing desires, these goals must therefore be relevant to him. If people are certain that the goals are their own, they do not fear that someone is using them to further that person's goals; this is a reason to set group goals by discussion. The discussion is not effective if the goals are nevertheless still established according to a previous plan. I can still remember an incident which occurred when I was about ten years old. My Sunday school teacher decided that we should have a name for our class. None of us cared much about it, but we agreed in order to please him. After some discussion we settled on a name which he suggested; we were henceforth to be known as the "Boaz Class." Later, we noticed that he had already written that name on the records, apparently before the beginning of class. Needless to say, our class never was very close to the teacher after that; we felt that we had been manipulated or at least taken for granted.

In the famous Hawthorne studies, which were conducted at the Hawthorne plant of Western Electric and reported by Roethlisberger and Dickson (1939), it was discovered that when workers thought the management was interested in their welfare they developed a new social orientation. No matter what physical changes the management instituted, production still increased. The physical conditions were not as important as the perceived motivation behind the change. Because the workers concluded that the change was brought about by the management's interest in them, they responded favorably to it. The key to secure the cooperation of a subject is therefore to convince him that you have a sincere interest in his welfare. The best way to do this is actually to have his best interests at heart. I once heard a lecture by a well-known labor arbitrator in which he said that he had never been involved in a case which could not have been solved by mutual concern of both parties for each other and by the desire of each to protect the rights of the other party.

Some people unfortunately need to build up their own self-esteem by tearing others down. These people point out faults "for your own good." Or they may provoke an argument with someone who is not in a position to fight back. One such person sticks in my mind, although I would like to forget him. One summer vacation from high school I was working behind a lunch counter, along with a number of other high school students. Although we served early breakfast, there was a rule against serving eggs to any customer after 10:00 A.M. because we were by then too busy with lunches. This rule did not stop one old man from coming in every day, in the early afternoon, and ordering eggs. As soon as he was given the daily response that we could not serve him eggs, he would loudly call for the manager, attracting everyone's attention. The manager, to stop the disturbance, always gave permission to serve the eggs. The customer then went through a little I-told-you-I-could-get-eggs routine, obviously enjoying his victory over the unlucky waiter. I never could understand why the manager did not issue a blanket permission to serve the man eggs at any hour. Perhaps it was because he did not want to deprive a steady customer of his daily pleasure.

The above story illustrates the principle that the public loss of face can be a very unpleasant experience. Witness the fact that I have remembered it so well for over twenty-five years! Unfortunately, we often see persons thoughtlessly embarrass or humiliate a child or a worker for some minor or imagined error without apparently realizing that the consequences can be long-term indeed.

The problem of self-esteem implies that a person should not be forced into taking a position from which retreat would cause him to lose face with other people. The situation should be arranged to prevent the person from initially making the incorrect response. The idea is to guide his behavior early enough so that he will never take the undesired position. There are two cautions here: do not overdo this, because if you are obvious you will antagonize the person, and also hinder his development of self-esteem. On the other hand, do not become a doormat to help your subject feel important, because he may lose respect for you as a result.

Pressure and coercion are not conducive to effective guidance, partly again because the person forced to do something loses self-esteem. In industry, for example, autocratic handling of workers causes the production to go down and stay down. A story in the newspaper some years ago described a man, visiting the zoo, who was ordered by a keeper to keep his child behind the safety rail in front of the lions' cage. The man then deliberately put his child over the rail, saying that the keeper could not tell them what to do. The child was then badly mauled by a lion. The man sacrificed his child's safety in order to prove his independence from the keeper. Thus, some people are likely to give an exaggerated negative and aggressive response to authoritarian rules and treatment. They have other desires, in other words, than to abide by rules. It is sadly ironic that some people are so negativistic that their behavior is almost completely determined by others. They do precisely what they are told *not* to do.

Nevertheless, individual differences are important, because people react to authoritarianism differently. Some become more submissive, whereas others become more aggressive.

Mechanisms of Motivation

A convenient general description of the motivational process is provided by what George Mandler (1962) has called the "jukebox theory." It compares a person to a jukebox, which can be turned on by inserting a coin. Without the coin, the machine has no capacity to do the thing for which it was designed—namely, to play a record. The coin energizes, or arouses, the machine to perform the appropriate act. We sometimes say of a person who is lazy and passive that he "needs to have someone put a nickle in him." This is a holdover from the days when a nickle could turn on a jukebox! The first part of an existing motivation therefore is the arousal or activation of the machine to perform.

Sometimes the person has the capability to perform a certain act, but not sufficient motivation. Adequate motivation (arousal) must be added before he can accomplish an act. This point is illustrated by the following story attributed to Billy Graham:

> A man was walking through a graveyard late one night and fell into an open grave. After repeated futile attempts to get out, and receiving no answers to his call for help, he curled up into one corner of the grave and went to sleep. Some time later another man fell into the grave and did not notice the first one. His repeatedly unsuccessful efforts to get out woke up the first man who tapped him on the shoulder and said, "You'll never get out." But he did!

The second part of the "motivation" of the jukebox to perform is provided by an input to the mechanism which selects the specific record to be played. In the case of a person, the mechanism selects which particular act is to be performed from all of the possible acts that the person could do. For example, a person may become aroused by having a practical joke played on him. Whether he chooses to be amused by it, or whether he becomes angry, depends upon the selector mechanism. Whether or not the joker is considered a friend probably controls the selection of either a friendly or a hostile response.

This selection mechanism is, of course, closely involved with the personality of the person. In fact, his type of personality is defined by which acts he characteristically selects. A hostile personality is one that is characterized by the frequent selection of hostile acts, whereas the friendly personality typically selects friendly acts.

Arousing Conditions

The "coin" that activates the human machine is some departure from a healthy, balanced state of the various need conditions within the body. Certain regulatory processes maintain the level of arousal within the preferred limits by mechanisms which reduce a need when it becomes too great. Therefore, we would say that the person would be motivated to reduce the need, and that he had a desire for the incentive that would reduce the need.

This departure from the balanced state within the person may be in his physical functioning or in his psychological functioning. The arousing condition could be some aspect of a stimulus input, like its meaning produced through previous learning. For example, a person could be aroused by being called a name that he considered offensive. Another person might not be offended by being called that name, perhaps because he did not understand the meaning of it. The word could have been the slang of one ethnic group which was not understood by a person from a different ethnic background. The reverse could also occur, because someone could be offended by a term that the speaker did not know was offensive. Thus, an external stimulus could be arousing because it had been associated with either a very pleasant or very unpleasant experience.

Certain situations would likely be either pleasant or unpleasant to most people because different persons would have had similar experiences. For example, most people would not desire to see vomit, whereas they would enjoy the sight of Mom's vegetable soup.

The arousing situation does not have to be a physical stimulus. It might even be a thought which occurs to the person as part of a train of thought, unrelated to existing stimulus input. The person may remember some act that he was going to perform. He might decide that it has been some time since he went fishing, for example. Or he might get an idea for an invention.

Finally, any unexpected input which catches the person by surprise could be arousing. The best example of this is startle, produced by an unexpected input, like a clap of thunder, or even a person suddenly touching you lightly on the shoulder when you are in deep thought about something else. Obviously one should avoid walking up silently or slamming a door behind someone who is working with a sharp instrument.

The stimulus is arousing primarily because it is unexpected. Often, in fact, the arousal created by a strong stimulus can be reduced by merely preparing the person for it. For example, the fearful child can be alerted when the mother anticipates that a crash of thunder is coming.

In the case of physical functions, the return to the balanced state of needs would be important in supporting life. An example of a fatal imbalance would be an excessive lack of oxygen in the blood because the person's supply of air was limited. The departure from the desired state leads to an increased level of arousal in the person, increasing to panic in the extreme case, plus immediate actions to gain more air. A swimmer would swim to the surface to breathe; the mountain climber would breathe faster because the air was thinner; the sinus-sufferer would take a blast of his favorite medicine up his nose. In short, some act of adjustment or coping with the environment would be required to satisfy the desire brought about by the physical need. It would very probably be made immediately if the lack were severe.

In the case of psychological functioning, the immediate survival of the person may not be at stake, although a prolonged psychological lack could lead to death, either directly or indirectly. For example, the person might be driven to suicide, or might die from a bleeding ulcer caused by worry, or he might have a fatal heart attack because he is grossly overweight as a result of overeating because of a psychological problem.

Whether or not the psychological imbalance is related to survival, it can still create a departure from the desired state of arousal, sometimes sufficiently to produce the undesired situation of extreme arousal called stress. Examples of conditions causing such stress would be homesickness, boredom, and frustration caused by the absence of familiar input—not so much what stimulation is present, but what is not present. Boredom refers, therefore, to the sameness of inputs—to the dominance of expected or previously experienced inputs. Thus, the absence of stimulating input, like excessive stimulation, can be unpleasantly arousing to the person. The person seeks a level of stimulus input that will keep his level of arousal within the limits which he personally desires.

The maintenance of a proper level of arousal could therefore require either an increase or decrease in environmental stimulation. A noisy factory or office might require some acoustical treatment to decrease the high level of noise. But another working area might be too quiet, requiring a little background music to keep the workers happy. As usual, individual differences enter the picture, because some workers may prefer more quiet, and others more stimulation.

Selector Mechanisms

The input to the motivational system which controls the selection of a response again could be a stimulus from outside the body or from inside, or from the activity of the mind. The external stimulus might be a printed sign saying "Free refreshments," "Heated pool," or "Palms read." It might also be the pressure of a tight shoe, or the failure of the air conditioning in hot weather. Each of these stimuli might cause equal amounts of arousal in a person, but probably cause him to do one act instead of another, as appropriate to the input. Examples of stimulus input from within the body would be contractions from an empty stomach, dryness of the mouth, or a headache. These situations would cause a person to eat, drink, or take an aspirin, respectively.

Some other desires can be satisfied in any of several ways. For example, a relief from boredom can be achieved by a vacation in the mountains, a trip to the seashore, or an ocean cruise. The office worker can spend time in his garden, or the farmer may go sight-seeing in the city. A factory worker may remain on the job but be given variety in the assigned jobs—spending one hour per day on eight jobs, if possible, instead of building up boredom on one job per day for eight hours. The coffee break obviously has the advantage of relieving both boredom and fatigue.

Effects of Strength

The strengths of the desires are important. The typical relationship which is found between strength of desire to produce an act and the effectiveness of that act is illustrated in figure 6-1. Starting from the extreme left at the bottom of the graph, and moving toward the right, increases of strength of desires are represented from very low to very high. The strength of act produced by each strength of desire is shown by the vertical length of the bar above each indicated strength of desire, measured by the scale at the left which runs from low to high. The graph shows therefore that as strength of desire increases from very low to very high, the strength of the act increases at first until it reaches the highest level and then it progressively decreases. Therefore, to perform a response best a person should have a medium degree of arousal; motivation which is too strong or too weak does not permit the best performance.

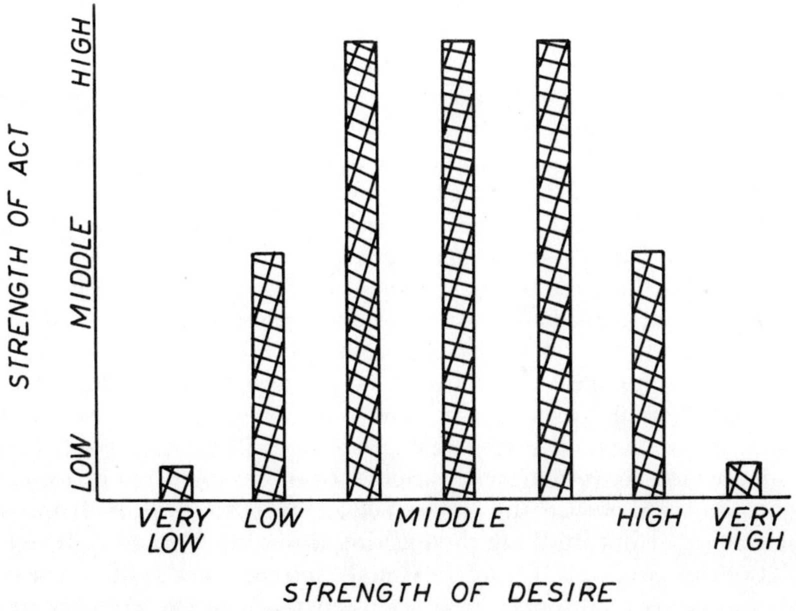

Figure 6-1. Illustration of the general relationship between various strengths of desire and the strength of the act, for an act that is not well learned.

Finding the Optimum

The importance of the above relationship cannot be stressed too much. A person will perform poorly if he tries too hard or not hard enough. The lesson to be learned from this by parents, teachers, and foremen is that the slow learner, or the poor producer, may have a problem of too much desire, instead of too little. Although he may well be undermotivated and need "to have a fire lit under him," he may on the other hand have too much "fire" under him already. He may need to relax because he is already too aroused. The proper approach of the guide to improve the performance is quite different depending upon which problem the person has. Often students do not perform well on a test because they panic, not because they are stupid or lazy. They become blocked or frozen with anxiety about the test.

High arousal leads to a sameness or stereotypy of behavior—a locking-in on one response which might well not be the correct one. This makes it very hard for the person to engage in productive thinking or any other creative act. When a person "hits the panic button" he is likely to perform like the novice automobile driver who is stuck in the mud or snow. The novice presses on the accelerator as hard as he can, in an attempt to get the auto to move ahead. But all he gets is spinning of his wheels. Less pressure on the accelerator would give the slower-moving wheels more chance to gain traction, and thus to deliver the required performance.

As an advisor to college students for many years, I have reached the conclusion that most of the college students who bring their problems to their advisors, or to the college counselling center, are those who are trying too hard. Their parents are putting pressure on them to achieve something, and they are trying to please their parents. Of course, the students who are lazy, or do not care about their parents, would not bother to come in for advice or counselling.

Some ways to increase the motivation—arousal level—of the subject-person have been discussed above. Now some ways to reduce the arousal level for persons with the opposite problems will be discussed. Obviously, if a person is overaroused, either by overstimulation or by exciting thoughts, he can reduce the arousal level by getting away from the stimulation or by not thinking the exciting thoughts. He can reduce the stimulation by going on a brief personal "retreat" to a spot where the stimulation is low. This may be a secluded place in the country, or a library, or a chapel. The chapel would be doubly effective because it would be easier there, through prayer and meditation, to drive disturbing thoughts from the mind by replacing them with more tranquil ones. Of course, reading in the library or praying in the country are other viable possibilities.

Permissiveness of expression tends to reduce tension in people. By letting a person talk about his feelings, you not only learn more about him, you also reduce his level of arousal. Tensions built up by various stresses are likely to produce responses, such as aggression, which probably will be very nonadaptive.

Many persons today reduce their arousal level by turning to drugs which tranquilize. Such drugs are obviously helpful when prescribed by a physician to relieve a temporary condition brought on by some current problem. They do not solve the problem itself, but they may prevent further complications due to the overarousal which was produced by the problem. This method can hold the person together until he can get the immediate problems solved, either by himself, or with medical, psychological, or other help.

If the sedated person does not solve the problem, however, the situation changes. A person who is always tranquilized gains a different set of problems. He needs to be aroused enough to accomplish certain necessary jobs. For example, a family friend was taking tranquilizers to help her through some personal problems. She reported that she did not worry about the problems anymore, but she also failed to worry about such things as whether or not her children got breakfast before they went off to school.

Apparently, this is one of the reasons why so many housewives start to take other kinds of drugs, which stimulate rather than calm them. They take "uppers" in the morning in order to be able to get the children off to school and "downers" so that they can get through the rest of the day. It is easy to see how someone can get caught in this cycle, taking a pill to get through every new situation.

The same kind of reasoning would apply to the person who got started on drugs for the opposite reason. A person might have some problem which caused apathy or depression and which might be helped by a physician's prescription for a stimulant. Again, the drug would not solve the basic problem, but it might help the person through a trying time. If the problem continues, however, we might ask what there is about the situation or personality of the person that makes him so continuously bored or depressed that he needs drugs to help him adjust to life. Again, the problem must eventually arise for the person: how is he to find a way to handle situations that cannot be successfully handled when he is "high"?

Importance of Task

Bindra (1959) points out that the appearance of the results in figure 6-1 would vary somewhat depending upon the particular task that the person was to perform. For different tasks the entire distribution of bars would be shifted either to the right or to the left. For a task that required strength and explosive energy—like weight lifting or heavy construction—the best levels of arousal would be higher, even though there would still be some highest level of arousal that would result in poorer performance. A task such as typing would ordinarily require a medium level of arousal for best performance. A task like creative thinking would, however, be done best at a relatively low level of arousal—keeping in mind, of course, that if the arousal gets too low no work at all will be done.

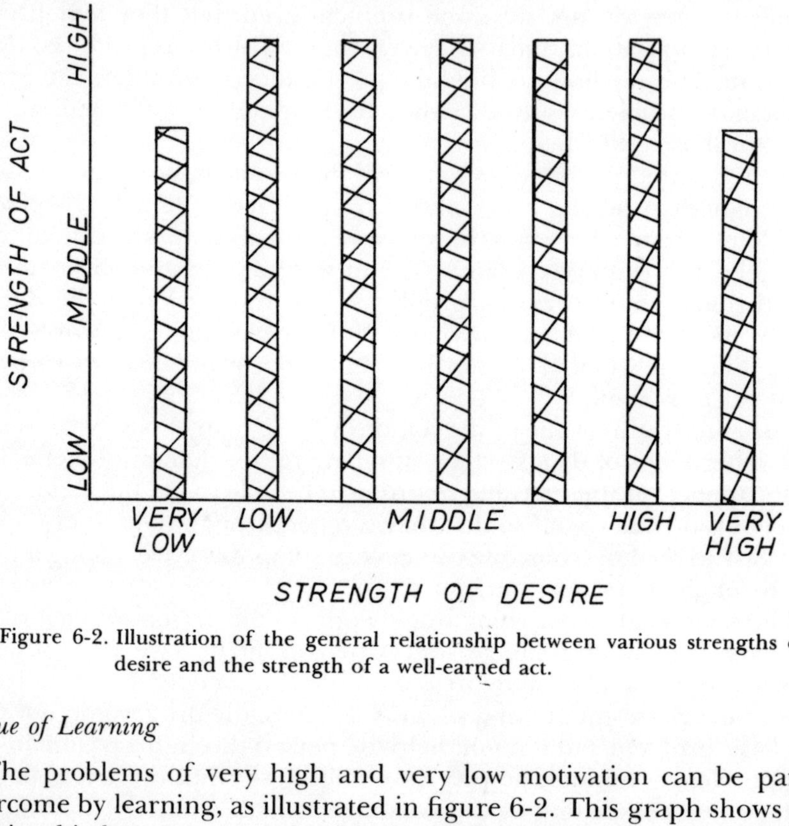

Figure 6-2. Illustration of the general relationship between various strengths of desire and the strength of a well-earned act.

Value of Learning

The problems of very high and very low motivation can be partly overcome by learning, as illustrated in figure 6-2. This graph shows the relationship between strength of desires and strength of act, when the act has been very well learned. There are still decreases at extreme degrees of arousal, but they are not nearly as great as with acts that are not well learned. Therefore, the person's ability to perform the act is high for almost all strengths of desires. Also the strength of the act is higher for each level of desire. The facts of figure 6-2 mean that learning to perform better than necessary "just to get by" will pay off when problems of too much or too little arousal appear. Even if one does not feel much like working, he can adequately perform the well-learned act. Not only that, but he can also perform the act when the pressure is on, and he must do well. For example, a highly skilled typist can turn out good copy quickly without paying too much attention to it, and he can also do an equally good job with the boss standing behind him to snatch the copy from the typewriter as soon as it is finished. Similarly, students will be much less likely to become overly nervous, and block the answers from their minds, if they know the material well. If they have "crammed" for the examination, working under pressure, the learning will not be as efficient. Also, if they are not confident of their mastery of the material, they are much more likely to have their minds go blank when it really counts.

Summary

This chapter first pointed out that understanding the desires of another person gives us the means to guide his behavior. Suggestions about methods to discover the desires of a person were offered. The key was to examine the acts of the person in order to see what goals he typically works for under specified conditions. Some desires result from physical structure and others from learning. The specific methods of satisfying the desires are often determined by learning, and thus can differ for different people. The concept of incentives indicates that the desirability of a reward depends upon the context and the experience of the person.

The motivational mechanisms of a person were compared to the mechanisms of a jukebox, which is first aroused to perform by some input—usually a coin. Then a selector mechanism determines the goal of the behavior—the tune to be played. For the person, the arousal occurs when there is an imbalance in the mechanisms which regulate the physiological and psychological processes. The goal of the behavior is determined by the nature of the imbalance, and what it signifies to the person. The relationship between strength of desire and adequacy of performance is described by an inverted U-shape. Thus, either too much or too little arousal does not produce best performance.

7. Personal Views

"Put yourself in his shoes." This advice means that to understand a person's reaction to a situation, it helps to try to see the situation as if you were looking at it from where he is standing. Different views of a situation can easily produce different reactions to it.

An illustration of an effect of a different physical point of view is the reaction of the "grandstand quarterback." It is obviously easier to see what the quarterback should do with the ball from high in the grandstands above the fifty-yard line than it is to make that determination from behind the line of scrimmage on the playing field. An apt saying, and one which refers to the skill of the "Monday morning quarterback," is that "hindsight is better than foresight." The more advantageous point of view is often from some distance, either in temporal or spatial perspective.

The difference is not just in terms of the physical view, but in relation to other factors, such as physical distractors. The kibitzer has none of the stresses which make the decisions of the participant more difficult. The observer on the sidelines is not running the risk of failure, nor can he hear the footsteps of the opposing players.

The idea of differences in viewpoint can be extended, of course, to refer figuratively to the differences in personal codes or frames of reference, which determine what meaning each person attaches to various inputs. It includes the person's ideas about what behaviors are proper or improper, as in a code of conduct. To the extent that the person's point of view is consistent, and this point of view influences his behavior, his acts will be consistent from one occasion to another. Different people can be described by whether or not they hold on to stable views or whether they change their views like their shirts when their personal interests are at stake.

This individualized point of view, or code, influences the perceptions and thus the responses of the person. For example, one of my former ministers told of receiving two letters from different visitors to a particular church service. One man wrote that he had enjoyed the worship service and that the people of the church were very friendly. The other said the church was cold and unfriendly. Although these two persons had attended exactly the same service, their personal perceptions of it were quite different, probably because of personality differences in the persons themselves.

Thus, the way information is translated into the personal code can affect the ability of persons to perceive, to learn, to remember, and to adjust. Inputs which we do not have the proper background to encode, possibly because we have not had sufficient prior experience with them, are difficult for us to discriminate among, and to remember. Thus, we are not likely to respond to them adaptively. For example, the person who has always been rich does not fully understand poverty, nor does a man fully appreciate the meaning of "Women's Lib."

Perceptual Effects

Because the views of a person influence how he perceives an event, the meaning is largely in the mind of the perceiver, so to speak, not completely a product of the input. It is determined by the coding category to which the person assigns the stimulation, thereby establishing its meaning.

Kinds of Distortion

Three kinds of distortion in perception are usually identified: illusion, delusion, and hallucination. Each of them involves an error in interpreting the environment.

Illusions A person is known by the kinds of perceptual distortions he makes. An illusion is an incorrect perception of a stimulus—seeing something in it, or about it, that is not objectively correct. We usually try to put some meaning into each stimulus input, even if the stimulus has no meaning of itself. We often add meaning, as in the case of a fleecy cloud or an inkblot which may suggest a meaningful form. Figure 7-1 shows an inkblot which was made by dropping a bit of ink on a blank sheet of paper, folding the paper at the ink, and pressing down. Although the blot is therefore meaningless, it can suggest different meaningful forms to different people. Probably many people will think that this one resembles a butterfly. We can use any idiosyncratic meaning that is attached to the meaningless figure by the person as a way of finding out what views he characteristically takes. We attempt to see what things look like from inside his shoes, so to speak. A single unusual response is not very important, however; only consistent unusual responses indicate a characteristic point of view of the person.

Figure 7-1. Illustration of a meaningless blot of ink, which often reminds persons of something meaningful.

Delusions Another way we tell something about a person is to examine any persistent delusions he might have. A delusion occurs when the person perceives literally and actually everything that has occurred, but assigns an incorrect meaning to it. For example, a person may see two people talking on a street corner and erroneously conclude that they are plotting against him.

Other delusions are not so striking, or so serious. They might be as simple as a man thinking a girl wants to become friends because she once spoke to him in a friendly manner, when in fact she was merely trying to be pleasant. Note that a belief is only a delusion if it is in error. The delusion can tell us about a person because the content of the delusion is ordinarily determined by his views and desires. Frequent and persistent delusions, held in spite of ample evidence against them, indicate abnormal psychological states in the person.

Hallucinations Hallucinations also can tell us about a person's views. These occur when there is no corresponding stimulation, and most of the person's sensation at the time is, in a sense, manufactured in his mind. These can occur in the normal person even under normal conditions; anybody can make a mistake. An example of this would be to think that you catch sight of something out of the corner of your eye when there is nothing there, or to think that you heard the telephone ring when it did not. You can demonstrate a hallucination to yourself by staying for several minutes in a completely light-tight room—a closet at night, for example. You will perceive that small spots of light flicker on now and then. These come from normal spontaneous activity in your nervous system—not as responses to any external stimulation.

Persistent hallucinations are characteristic of abnormal states, such as mental illness or drug intoxication. The most familiar illustration of this would be the apparently frequent appearance of pink elephants to the alcoholic.

Adaptational State

Our attitudes, prejudices, and expectations are controlled by what we are accustomed to in our society. For example, the attitudes of the people in our society about things such as emotional problems, marital problems, etc., influence the way we view them. What we are most accustomed to therefore becomes what we consider the natural state of affairs, or the normal response. Our expectations often lead to "self-fulfilling prophecies;" we *make* things come out the way that we *expect* them to turn out.

The parent or teacher who is accustomed to normal children may have expectations which are too high for a retarded child or for a slow-learning class. This also can work in reverse. One teacher of retarded children told me how he thought that *all* his pupils were doing well until he had occasion to observe a class of normal children. My wife, as a teacher in special education, spent a lot of time with learning-disabled children. She did not realize how much this carried over to her dealings with our own normal children until one day our son, who was about eight years old at the time, asked her why she said, "Come, Payten, come," when they were downtown together. She was so used to communicating with her schoolchildren in the simplest language possible that she had carried it over to her dealings with her own children. Needless to say, our son did not appreciate her lack of discrimination.

Effects of Desires

The desires of a person also affect what he perceives. He attends selectively to the stimuli around him, depending upon his desires. In a sense, he manufactures his own personal environment—what some psychologists call his "life space." He notices some things and not others. We can say that the nature of the world about him is in his own eye, the eye of the beholder.

This short-term selectivity of attention is called a "set." For example, if a person is travelling on the highway and is hungry, then he is set to see the hamburger sign. As soon as he has located such a sign and has eaten, then he is more likely to pay attention to other, different stimuli.

The qualitative nature of such sets, and their frequency and persistence, defines the basic personality of the person. If we say that a person consistently desires some things, then he consistently perceives in this manner. Thus we can say our views are tuned by our own interests and desires. We are most familiar with this in the refereeing of athletic contests. We see the errors that our opponents make but not the errors that our own team makes. We do not have a readily available category of judgment for the information that, "our man fouled," or "our side cheats." This is why referees are ordinarily selected to be nonpartisan. Generally, both teams try to select a referee who does not have a particular bias for or against either team. Often charges of bias are made, of course. There was a story in our local newspaper some years ago that after a high school basketball game, when someone asked the referee who won, he replied, "we did." As you can imagine, the losers were quite upset about this interpretation of the outcome.

There are a number of general rules to determine what stimuli will be likely to catch one's attention. For example, most persons tend to remember aspects of tasks that are uncompleted, rather than completed. Also, most people tend to remember pleasant experiences, rather than unpleasant ones. However, there are exceptions to these generalities, depending upon the personality of the person. Some persons remember defeats; others remember their victories.

Some people have developed consistent views which they hold in spite of changing desires. Others have not; their views are entirely determined by what they want. For example, a person may view economic inflation somewhat differently depending upon whether he is trying to buy or wanting to sell. When we refer to such cases of changes in views with changes in desires, we use the common expression, "the shoe is on the other foot." Obviously, the person who can only adopt views in terms of his own immediate desires will not have the flexibility of thinking to be an effective problem-solver or to get along well with others.

Conclusions

This above discussion implies that meaning attached to an input is not really in the external stimulus itself, but in the way that it is coded in the mind of the perceiver. All the perceiver, or receiver, of input can be directly aware of is the activity in his own nervous system. From this, he makes some inferences about what external object or situation is most likely to have produced this pattern of neural activity which he now experiences in his brain.

This means, to be sure, that a person can obtain a correct perception on the basis of only partial information in the input situation. From fragmentary information he can construct a complete and accurate perception. It also means that even under the impact of very much information from the stimulus situation he may however reach a false conclusion about the true identity of the object or situation. This point is particularly important in evaluating the truthfulness of an eyewitness report of a crime or other significant happening. Such reports are notoriously unreliable. Eyewitnesses are likely to perceive what they expect to perceive, and to remember the interpretation they have already put on what they perceived.

The above point is also most relevant to the problem of drugs in our society, particularly in the case of the so-called mind-expanding drugs. The user may reach the conclusion that he is perceiving the reality of the external environment particularly well. However, it is not possible for him to know whether he is perceiving more accurately, or whether his perceptions are in error and he actually has a misconception (delusion) that he is perceiving truth more accurately.

Effects on Memory

The distortions of memory shown by a person can also tell us something about his internal state of affairs, about what codes for inputs he has available to him. For example, what details does he tend to miss or to forget, and what details does he tend to emphasize in memory? A famous experiment by Carmichael, Hogan, and Walter (1932) illustrates well the importance of the name given to an input and its effect upon how it is encoded into memory. Their experimental subjects tended to remember nonsense shapes differently, depending upon what name had been given to each figure when it was first shown to them. If the figure had been called, for example, a barbell, it tended to appear like a barbell in a later reproduction. On the other hand, if the same figure had been called eyeglasses, the reproduction tended to look more like spectacles. The name given to each figure caused it to be viewed differently. The way it was coded influenced how it was later reproduced from memory.

The answer then to the question, "What's in a name?", is that in a name is the sum total of the ideas or codes associated in our minds with that name. We give the named object the attributes associated with the name, and we tend to remember our own code name, not the original object itself. A recent article in the newspaper reported that in one region of the country a man was favored on a ballot for public office if his surname had a Scandinavian sound to it, but was at a definite disadvantage if his name sounded Italian. This unfair coding of a man's credentials, discriminating on the basis of his name and not his deeds, probably resulted from the fact that the Mafia originated in Sicily, far away from Scandinavia.

Effects on Responses

The person's views are manifested also through their effects on his responses. Sigmund Freud (1943) studied mistakes in output—as in slips of the tongue—for this purpose. According to Freud, errors of perception, memory, or responding were due to conflicts in the internal workings of the mind. Slips of the tongue (or typewriter) provide the easiest illustrations of such output errors. Some years ago a newspaper apologized for a previous error as follows:

> In yesterday's paper we printed through typesetter's error a notice about the *defectives* on the police force, when we meant of course the *detectives*. We regret the error and submit our apologies to the detectives on the police farce.

Freud would argue that it was not accidental that the writer substituted the word "farce" for the intended word "force" in the last line. We might well wonder about the writer's opinion of the police in his city. This idea that our actions can betray our true "feelings" or views, in spite of our attempts to hide them, comes up repeatedly in this book. It was extensively discussed in connection with minimal cues in chapter 5.

Generalization and Discrimination

We now come again to the problems of generalization and discrimination which are central to psychology. They were discussed in the context of input in chapter 5. Whereas generalization refers to giving responses that are the same to different stimulus inputs, discrimination refers to giving different responses to the different inputs. This chapter is concerned with the generalization and discrimination processes in terms of the conceptual or categorizing behaviors of the subject-person. Thus, two inputs are perceived by the person as either belonging to the same category (generalization), or as belonging to different categories (discrimination).

Similarity and Dissimilarity

Obviously, it is easier to respond similarly to two inputs when they are similar, and to respond to them differently when they are dissimilar. Unfortunately, it is impossible to define what similarity is for a given person in a given situation. It depends upon the experiences he has had; he will have his own personal concepts and, therefore, will tend to see things differently from persons who have had different experiences. When two inputs are coded as belonging to the same concept by that person, they are by this act defined in his view as similar.

A striking case in point was the reaction of the United States government to Japanese-American citizens early in World War II. Because these citizens looked like Japanese, many of them were treated unfairly and inappropriately, as if they were more Japanese than American. It is interesting that German-Americans were not similarly treated. Probably part of the difference was that the physical appearance of citizens of German descent was less distinguishable from that of other Americans.

Two inputs may be very much alike in terms of physical attributes, but still be coded by the individual as different, however. Some small detail of discriminated difference may cause the difference in response. Just the name given to an object can affect its desirability. I remember as a child enjoying a dinner of "marsh rabbit," only to be distressed after dinner to find out that the more common name for the main dish was "muskrat." Then, as now, a "rabbit" fit into my coding system as something edible, whereas a "rat" did not. To be sure, someone else would not consider the rabbit meat to be dinner food, and so it goes.

Another illustration concerns the coded meaning of a single attribute of a person. When my son was very young, he referred to a good friend of our family as being a "brown person," although she was in fact a Caucasian with dark skin. No wonder a child is confused when our society identifies a person as being "white," "black," or "brown," when actually we are not referring to his skin color at all.

Two inputs may, on the other hand, be formally quite dissimilar, but may be perceived as similar because of certain of the person's experiences. We have all had the experience of disagreeing with another person about whether or not two persons look alike. Sometimes, also, one person will remind you of another, but you yourself will not really know what causes you to think that they are similar in appearance.

A common psychological experience for probably everyone is what psychologists call *déjà vu*—French words meaning "already seen." The person has the strong feeling that he has previously experienced a view or event, but knows that he is actually experiencing it for the first time. For example, he may travel to a distant place, where he has never been, and encounter, let us say, a hotel and has the feeling of having seen it before. The most likely explanation for this is that he has seen a similar hotel somewhere which strongly reminds him of this one or that he has seen parts of several different buildings which, when combined in memory, remind him of the present structure.

Value of Generalization

There are, of course, times when it is appropriate to respond to different stimuli as if they were the same. For example, a person would tend to treat someone else's mother in much the same way that he has learned to treat his own. One would be able to conclude that a Ford or Chevrolet, or some unfamiliar new model, were all automobiles capable of providing transportation.

Generalization also implies the carrying over, or transfer, of learning from one situation to another. Therefore, one would want to have his child, student, or worker show evidence of carrying over the beneficial learning which originally occurred in the home, classroom, or training program to other applied situations for which the learning was undertaken.

Value of Discrimination

There are times, on the other hand, when it is important to distinguish between different categories, for example, when you are looking for your own automobile in the parking lot, or intending to give your wife a little intimate pat at a party. It can be embarrassing and dangerous if you drive the wrong car or pat the wrong wife.

Particularly in recent years, we have heard that discrimination is bad. This is not always so. I have shocked audiences at parent-teacher meetings several times by stating that I am in favor of discrimination. A person should be discriminating in his choices; he should never act indiscriminately. The problem for the person is to know when to generalize and when to discriminate. The important goal here, however, is to discriminate on the basis of relevant and important differences. For example, if one tends to think in stereotypes, making statements like "all black people are jolly" and "all Irishmen have fiery tempers," then he cannot readily perceive the moody black or the calm Irishman. Therefore, education must provide adequate experience for the person to enable him to take different views and to avoid such stereotypes in his thinking. His categories of judgment or coding of inputs should not be so limited that he has no available category into which he can fit the true state of affairs.

Stereotypes are not always about bad characteristics. They can also produce what psychologists call the "halo effect" mentioned earlier in chapter 5. In this phenomenon, a person having some desired attribute is erroneously perceived as having other desired attributes. For example, a suitor may be blind to the faults of his lady love, or a parent may find it difficult to see the shortcomings of his own child, as described in the expression "love is blind."

The person who is successful in interpersonal relations has developed his capacity to discriminate between the stimuli to which he should be blind and those that he should perceive. A parent who is blind to a problem of his child will not be able to help the child. On the other hand, a parent who carps on minor faults will magnify existing problems and possibly create new ones. We must learn when to be blind and when to be perceptive.

Conception of Self

The concept of self is the view that a person has of himself. A general motivation of people is for ego expansion—that is, to enhance their conception of themselves, to build self-esteem. A person will perform acts in order to protect his self-esteem, to "save face." Therefore, we should try to prevent a person from expressing a position of view which later will have to be given up under force or other circumstances. If he has to "back down" later, he will "lose face," and thus self-esteem.

One way that the person assesses himself is through the reactions of others. Therefore, people need approval and praise from others. The more authoritative a person is believed to be, the more valued is his approval.

A person indicates his own assessment of himself by his actions. For example, a modern youth who deliberately presents the image of a hippie tells something about his view of himself. We can ask, "What is so important about how long and how dirty a person keeps his hair?" The important thing is that he is telling about his attitudes and philosophy of life; it is what the hairstyle means that is significant. As in the case of the Cavaliers and Roundheads of English history, one can judge with better than chance accuracy the person's political philosophy by whether he is wearing long curls or short hair.

Obviously, it would be foolish to feel confident that you know a person is politically liberal merely because he wears his hair long. On the other hand, he knows, as well as you do, that a person with long hair is more likely to be judged as liberal and antiestablishment. If this line of reasoning caused us to perceive a long-haired person as antiestablishment, in spite of ample evidence to the contrary, we would be showing stereotyped thinking and, in this case, suffering under a delusion.

Communication among Persons

One of the early reviewers of this book remarked that I showed a strong bias against hippies by assuming that they did not wash. She argued that some hippies do wash, and that I was overgeneralizing—not making a proper discrimination. My reply was that in my coding system anyone who washed was not a hippie; a freaky-looking person who washes is probably just a liberal person wearing funny clothes. Thus, many issues which seem to be differences of opinion are merely differences in definition. To avoid arguments, both parties should agree on what the words mean.

In order to communicate effectively with a person, it is necessary to understand his system for coding the input information. Therefore, one can code the input into a language that is appropriate for that person. Another way of saying this is that one puts the information in the concept system of the other person, or puts the information in the other's own words. One key to effective communication is to allow the person to recast the idea into his own words and then to repeat it back. If he does this satisfactorily, he has in fact properly coded the information.

If the guide is able to provide sufficient information to permit the person to arrive at the proper interpretation by himself, then the intake of information will be most effective. The person uses his own code to provide the meaning for the input; therefore, it should be maximally meaningful to him.

Different Codes

The views of a person are, of course, reflected by his personality. That is to say, his prevailing views are influenced by his motivations and by his previous experiences. Therefore, in a real sense, the person is always looking at the world through "personality-colored" glasses. The personality adds a tint to all of the person's perceptions and memories, just as looking through rose-colored glasses imparts a rosy view of the world. A personal experience fixed this idea in my mind. While spending a leave of absence in California one year, I remarked one day that the brown grass on the hills had started to turn green. The rest of my family disagreed with me, and an argument ensued until someone pointed out that I was wearing green-tinted glasses. When I took them off, the green fields of spring were gone.

It is only possible for a person to use those coding systems that he has learned. If a person has not experienced a given view, he is not likely to adopt it. This is best illustrated by the generation gap. While the youth has difficulty understanding the views of the parent, because he has not himself been a parent or had the same number of years of experience, the parent has the disadvantage of not having been a youth for many years, and also of having been a youth under quite different world conditions. The question naturally arises as to which generation has the more accurate perception of what the world is really like now. Unfortunately, each person tests the world according to his own frame of reference and personal views; it is never possible to communicate exactly what these are to any other person. A friend of mine was discussing with her young son her problems in trying to understand his point of view. "You know," she said, "I have never been a little boy." "But," he protested, "this is the first time that I have ever been a little boy." The young child has not had much time to develop a consistent point of view.

Often the same words mean different things to different people. This is particularly true if the people come from different age groups or ethnic backgrounds. I have been shocked a number of times myself by hearing younger people use words and phrases which were later revealed to have quite different meanings to them today than they had to me when I was their age. For example, in my youth, the phrase "making out" implied nothing short of full sexual intercourse. Imagine my shock when my children mentioned that some kids were "making out" on the school bus going to and from school. Apparently, this phrase today means nothing more than what we used to call "necking."

Many misperceptions of words in standard sayings are made by young children, sometimes with humorous results, because they have not had the background for understanding. For example, children have been known to perceive the line in the Lord's Prayer as "Harold be thy name," or, in the case of the Twenty-third Psalm, to understand it to say "good Miss Murphy," instead of "goodness and mercy." My favorite illustration of this is the hymn about "Gladly, the cross-eyed bear." The child does not know the proper verbal codes, and thus uses the only ones that he has available. Often small children embarrass their mothers by calling all men "daddy" because they do not know the word for "man."

Communication can be achieved, however, if sufficient attention is given to the problem of putting inputs into the proper language for translation by the receiver. This was concluded by a conference of people from many disciplines called in 1959 by the National Academy of Science to study long-range problems of improving the distribution of scientific knowledge in the United States. They concluded that whatever the stage of development of the child, he has his own views and codes of the world into which he translates his experiences to give them meaning. The task for guides is to translate their message into the coding language of the child, rather than asking the child to understand the thought forms of the adult world. In summary:

> The task of teaching a subject to a child at any particular age is one of representing the structure in terms of the child's way of viewing things (Bruner, 1960, p. 33).

Problems of communication can also arise between adults of different backgrounds and education. For example, many years ago a financial officer and I had difficulty in establishing an approved budget for my research grant. He wanted a "firm" budget, with "firm" estimates of costs. I was unwilling to say that certain figures were firm because many unforeseen events always pop up in the course of a year on a research project. Finally, I remarked that I would not know what to do if money were left in one category of a firm budget, but all of the money in another category had been spent. His reply was that the proper procedure in such a case was merely to write a letter transferring funds from one category to another. I immediately told him that my previously submitted budget was in fact "firm." Once we understood the same meaning for that word, our problem vanished.

Communications gaps also frequently occur between members of different races. To gain understanding of what it is to be black in a ghetto, a white person can darken his skin and live in a ghetto for a period of time. This will give the white some of the experiences of the ghetto blacks and put him in their shoes to some extent. But the situation cannot be exactly the same for such a person as it is for a genuine disadvantaged black. The fake knows that he can get out of the ghetto whenever he wants. He cannot experience the frustration and depression which would naturally come only from a realization that he had no choice in the future.

Need for Education

Enrichment or improvement in the ability to add meaning to input situations is obtained from varied experiences and from formal education. The child soon learns, for example, that the word "Daddy" means a particular man, because others laugh or become annoyed when he calls the mailman, milkman, or father's boss, "Daddy." The difference is quickly explained to him. Other more complex codes of meaning can be learned by similar methods.

Although a person can never truly understand what it is like to be in the other person's shoes, he can approach this state by various means. He can read accounts about a person in autobiographies or biographies; he can seek out the appropriate situation and observe it. He can ask questions, as young children most definitely do.

According to the present conception, the culturally disadvantaged are those who have not had an equal opportunity to develop rich, broad codes or frames of reference. They have had little opportunity to meet people from different backgrounds, to read many books, and to observe different environments. Therefore, they will ordinarily not be able to add as much meaning to as many input situations, or to make the discriminations and distinctions which are important for solving the new problems which they encounter outside of the ghetto. They will not be as skilled in communicating with other people, or learn as rapidly as the advantaged group. Such persons would therefore show up on conventional tests of intelligence as inferior to the person with more varied experience. The points of view and codes that they do have are not likely to be of much help on the standard test of intelligence, although they are probably very helpful for coping with their own environments.

This difference can work in reverse also. The privileged person may not understand the facts of life for the underprivileged. An excellent example of this is the classic remark which has been attributed to the French queen, Marie Antoinette, just before the French Revolution. She asked why the people were shouting and was told that they protested because they had no bread to eat. Her comment, "Then let them eat cake," is a classic example of the failure to understand the views of another.

For the person who has not had the opportunity to have many and varied experiences, there will frequently be emotional barriers also. The person is likely to be fearful and apprehensive about new and unfamiliar situations. Therefore, he will have more problems in coping with new situations because he is too emotionally aroused to learn readily.

In working with children, an advantage is often gained from having the lessons treated as games. In this way, the lessons are coded as something enjoyable rather than as drudgery. If the parent or teacher suggests that the activity will be enjoyable, the child expects fun. But if the adult implies that the lesson is a necessary evil, the child will be less likely to view it as enjoyable.

Choice of Views

One obvious way that a person develops his views is by identification with, or imitation of, his like-sexed parent. From this he learns many of his views of the opposite sex, for example. He will tend to identify with the person with whom he spends large amounts of time. The one who is imitated need not necessarily be a parent, but it is important, for example, that a fatherless boy have substantial amounts of contact with a man having strong masculine characteristics, who will be a good model for him to identify with and to imitate. If he does not have such a model, he may learn to be more like mother—inadequately prepared to accept a male role in life.

From this association with an adult model, the child develops his notions of what is right or wrong. These conceptions of right and wrong are necessary for the development of what we call the conscience. The conscience refers to an evaluation of an act with respect to whether or not it is in harmony with the views which are consistently held by the person—his personal code. There is a feeling of dissatisfaction with oneself when one has done something that is contrary to one's own personal views.

Some persons have not had the experiences which are necessary to develop a conscience, and therefore have developed what we call sociopathic personalities; they are people without conscience. They apparently do not have a personal code or view with respect to morally right or wrong activities in their own behavior. Other persons may, of course, acquire views that are quite different from those learned by the majority of persons in their society. Because they subscribe to a code of ethics, they are not sociopathic; neither are they necessarily incorrect in their beliefs merely because they are in the minority.

Another way of developing views is through identification and imitation of normal standards of the general society or culture. Different cultures have different views or standards of behavior. What is acceptable in one sub-group or culture is not always accepted in another. Some views are learned from other segments of society, in addition to those learned from parents.

The selection of standards to live by should be made by the person himself, rather than imposed by outside authority. For example, when parents try to impose their views on children, the result is often a conflict and miscommunication between the two. Parents do have some responsibility for the views that the child has selected, however, because they have control over many of the child's experiences. For example, the parents can indulge the child and allow him, therefore, to believe that he can get away with anything. Too often the parents build in one information translation or coding system for six years and then "send the kid to school to straighten him out," that is, to teach him discipline. The old saying that adversity builds character is true. The person who has grown up with few problems which require an adjustment of responses has had little opportunity to develop effective skills for coping with problems, and little experience in handling adjustively the subsequent frustrations.

If the views of an adult change drastically, it is probably because of experienced failure in achieving satisfaction of his desires by acting according to his prior views, or because of a deliberate attempt to educate himself to new and broader views. Chapter 10 discusses how views can be changed.

Summary

This chapter discusses the views of a person in terms of his coding of inputs in order to give them meaning. The codes vary for different people depending upon the different experiences. There are several kinds of distortions of coding. A person is likely to perceive what is convenient and pleasant for him to perceive, to ignore the unpleasant, and to fear the totally unfamiliar.

Problems of generalization and discrimination were discussed. The important job of the guide is to teach the proper basis for discriminating differences and for generalizing across similarities. Good interpersonal adjustment requires blindness to certain faults of others, as well as the discrimination of important differences. The need for a person to protect and enhance his view of himself should be recognized.

The use of different coding systems contributes to problems of communication between groups of people who have had different experiences. Examples of this are gaps between persons of different generations and between persons of different ethnic backgrounds. These problems require special efforts to translate all communications into the appropriate language or coding system of the intended receiver.

The choice of a frame of reference or code is conditioned by personal experience. First there is imitation of the parents and, later, conformity to society.

8. Personal Decisions

Between the input and the production of the response, specialized mechanisms translate the input information into the appropriate actions. These translations are not like the connections made by an operator on a telephone switchboard, which tend to be very simple by comparison. These complex connection-making mechanisms are the decision-making parts of the person, and form what we ordinarily call the "mind," as when we say, "make up your mind."

The selection of some of our responses requires virtually no use of the rational mind, however. These are the reflex responses that our body makes for us, so to speak. The appropriate stimulus consistently produces the act, even though a decision by the person was not required. For this reason, a reflex illustrates an extreme instance of what is known as "stimulus-bound behavior," behavior controlled primarily by the stimulus input. Examples of reflexes are the familiar knee jerk, which is achieved by a mild blow just below the kneecap when the person is sitting with his leg dangling. Another reflex is the quick withdrawal of the hand when it touches a hot object.

Because these responses do not require a decision by the person, he becomes aware of them only after he has made them, if indeed he is aware of them at all. A reflex is a protective device, because the individual can react even before he is consciously aware of a danger. A person moves his hand off a hot stove even before he is aware that he has been stimulated. If he had to wait long enough for his mind to reach a decision about whether or not to remove his hand, actual tissue damage would, of course, be likely.

Because the reflexes represent "mindless" responding, they produce generally about the same behaviors in all normal persons. Coping with these stimuli depends upon the normal functioning of the structures of the body, and therefore differences between individual persons with respect to these behaviors are relatively less important than those that involve decisions of the mind.

The decision that a person makes involving the use of the mind may be either conscious or unconscious. That is to say, he may be aware of the decision and of why he is making it, or he may be unaware of the basis for the decision. Examples of normally unconscious responses occur for certain vital functions which keep the person alive, such as breathing. One can breathe even though he is unconscious or asleep. Of course, he can consciously control his breathing for a period of time. A person might be able to hold his breath until he falls unconscious, at which time he will start to breathe again automatically. This is important for parents to remember when a young child threatens to hold his breath until he gets something he wants.

Some of the conscious decisions are so complicated that they are painfully slow. They may represent agonizing deliberations over a period of days or months. Others may be deliberately quick, such as the reaction of a football player to the snap of the ball, or of the boxer to the start of a blow by his opponent.

Each person is known by the type of decisions that he makes, because the decisions determine the actions. Thus, the development of the capabilities for making effective decisions means the maturing of the personality. For example, a person may respond to those stimuli which tend to give him pleasure immediately. This kind of reaction, characteristic of the very immature child, is what Sigmund Freud (1943) called responding to the "pleasure principle." On the other hand, an older child would be more inclined to respond according to what Freud called the "reality principle;" he may make a practical, reasoned response in terms of his views and understanding of the world, delaying immediate satisfaction for the achievement of more substantial long-term goals. This, of course, depends upon being more mature and more experienced, thus having more self-discipline. In this sense, a more experienced person implies a more- or better-educated person, in the broadest sense of the term "education."

The decisions of the individual result therefore from a balance between the insistent demands of the desires and the rational requirements of the views. The more mature and the better-educated person keeps a proper rein on the desires, and thus responds rationally. On the other hand, the very young, the undereducated, the retarded, or persons with other specific problems may have a greater tendency to respond to momentary desires. To have maturity means to give greater weight in the decision-making process to the views, and less to the satisfaction of desires that are not essential for life.

The young and the uneducated are thus more likely to respond to stimuli in ways which are intended to give them immediate pleasure. They are likely to behave in response to these stimuli in the same way that gave them pleasure in the past. Therefore, in other words, they are more "stimulus bound." In the language of Charles Silberman's book, *Crisis in the Classroom* (1970), the poorly educated person is more likely to make a mindless choice of a response. On the other hand, the more mature or educated person is less stimulus bound, and therefore more able to give appropriate different responses to any one particular input situation. Because his response is not completely determined by the stimulus input, he can evaluate outcomes of responses to particular stimulus situations and adjust his acts accordingly. He is more likely to take an analytic approach. He will try to test, either by performing test actions or by anticipation of outcomes in his mind, the effects of different responses to the same situation.

Effects of Experience

The decisions of a person are therefore strongly biased by his views, built through experience. They may be only slightly affected by the information in the stimulus input. The tendency for a person to read his own meaning into an unclear stimulus was discussed in chapter 7. A classic study by Wyatt and Campbell (1951) illustrates how this tendency to make inferences influences the conclusions reached by subject-persons when the stimulus input is unclear. In this study, lantern slides of meaningful scenes were shown to groups of students. The scenes were relatively common—a closeup view of a rose; a baby lying in a playpen; the face and upper body of a house cat; several pieces of laundry hanging in a tenement backyard. Some of the slides were shown at eight different stages of focus, in increasing order of clarity from very blurred to clear; other slides were shown just once at some isolated intermediate stage of unclear focus. The students revealed superior accuracy in perceiving the content of the isolated slides, which they had not previously seen at a more blurred focus. About one-half of the errors when the subjects had previously seen a slide were repetitions of earlier incorrect responses to it. Therefore these subjects were less accurate in their perception because presumably the previous unclear stimulation caused them to make false hypotheses or guesses about the contents of the slides. Because the contents of the slides were complex scenes, the subjects had the possibility of making many more incorrect hypotheses than correct ones. Having made these premature hypotheses, they tended to hold on to them even in the face of the additional information contained in the additional exposures of the slide in clearer focus.

The Wyatt and Campbell study raises the interesting idea that prior experience with a situation does not always lead to greater accuracy of the later conclusions. If the prior inconclusive experience fosters a jump to a premature conclusion and blinds the observer to further information to be gained later, causing him to hold on to the previous false interpretation, then the experience actually hinders performance in the subsequent tasks.

On the other hand, as so often happens in psychology, the above result depends upon certain critical facts about the testing situation. One of my own studies (Harcum, 1964) compared the perception of words after they had been exposed previously, but so rapidly that accurate perception of them was impossible, to the perception of new words, ones that had not appeared before in the experiment. The subjects were able to gain some information from the prior unclear perceptions that was usable later to improve the perception of the word. This illustrates again the problem of interaction—"it all depends"—mentioned in chapter 2. Whether prior incomplete information facilitates or hinders later accurate perception thus depends upon the particular type of stimulus inputs involved. Presumably, for the group of words that I used, prior perception of a few letters was likely to aid in the adoption of a correct hypothesis about which word had been exposed.

Intelligence

Experience is an important factor in the development of what we know as intelligence, an attribute which, of course, determines the effectiveness of decisions that a person makes for his own adjustment. The term "intelligence" is difficult to define because it implies several things. On the one hand, it refers to the inherited ability of a person to learn to solve problems and to reach other rational decisions. But it also means the final level of actualization of this first ability. This problem was clarified by D. O. Hebb (1949) who described what he called "intelligence A" and "intelligence B." By intelligence A, he meant the inherited capacity for learning and creative responding with which the person was born. This inherited characteristic sets limits on the final level of development of the intellectual capacity of the person. The developed intelligence B is what is actually measured on the standardized intelligence tests.

Proper experiences are required for the person to achieve the full actualization of his potential. At birth, the human infant is characterized by a notorious lack of intelligent behavior. He would die if he were not cared for by someone else. However, as he grows, his inherited potential unfolds in the maturation process. He can achieve a much higher level of intellectual performance than any other animal, because of the superiority of the human brain. There is an interaction with his environment such that varied experiences tend to aid in the development of the adult intelligence.

Since intelligence is a composite ability, the sum of several component abilities, certain aspects of it can be developed in one culture and not in another. A culture-free test would be one in which the performance would not depend upon the particular experiences that a person has had in his own culture. To date, however, it is doubtful that a culture-free test of intelligence has been achieved.

A measured level of intelligence within the normal range implies that the person initially had a normal level of intellectual ability, coupled with the usual experiences or education of a person in that population. The gifted child shows development which is accelerated in relation to normal children of his age, whereas the retarded child shows ability which lags behind that of the normal child of his age. The I.Q., or Intelligence Quotient, is based on this way of specifying intellectual ability. This measure is merely a description of the person's performance on a test, which purports to measure intellectual ability, with respect to other people of the same age who have had comparable experience. The intellectual capability of persons increases, of course, as they grow older, up to about sixteen years. The fact that the I.Q. remains approximately constant as the person grows older means that he is retaining his relative position with respect to the other people of his age who have been given the test.

The problem in assessing the true intelligence of a child who has not had "normal" experience—such as the black child of the urban ghetto—is that his inherited intelligence has interacted with impoverished experience in terms of the things that are necessary to score high on the typical intelligence test. Thus, a depressed development of intelligence B is measured by our standard intelligence tests, which presume "normal" experience, defined as the experience which the more advantaged child has enjoyed. Several persons have pointed out that the ghetto child may know as much as the advantaged child, but that the standard intelligence tests ask questions that tap information available to the advantaged child but less available to the disadvantaged child. Thus, as William Raspberry discusses in an article in *Newsweek* (1974) the disadvantaged child would score higher on an I.Q. test based on ghetto slang, because the test would be biased toward him rather than against him. Raspberry cites one of several such tests, developed by Robert Williams of Washington University, which illustrates this point. One item is as follows:

> *Nose opened* means: (a) flirting; (B) teed off; (C) deeply in love; (D) very angry.

In general, ghetto blacks know that the correct answer above is (C), whereas whites do not.

The person without the background experience that everyone else takes for granted can appear to be very stupid. An event from my boyhood illustrates this point. I grew up in a city, but each summer visited a farm. One summer on the farm I was sent to dig some potatoes but returned empty-handed; I had been unable to locate any because I did not know that potatoes grow on the roots of the plants instead of on the branches. Until that time I had not had the opportunity to learn what any farm boy learns at an early age. Therefore, the practical issue of intelligence is not so much what score a person makes on a test, but his ability to solve the problems in his own life situation. To be sure, however, the disadvantaged child who wishes to succeed in the general society must learn the things that are important in general society.

Reasoning

Because habits are the learned associations between stimuli and responses, they depend directly upon experience. Reasoning, on the other hand, is solving the problem by putting together two or more separate habits which have not been experienced together in the past. Reasoning thus does require experience in the sense that the person must have previously developed the individual habits which he later connects.

Insight is the process of suddenly finding the solution to a problem that one has been working on for some time. It also requires experience because one must first become familiar with all of the components that are later put together for the solution. Frequently, this requires a complete reorganization of a person's perception of the problem.

Types of Conflict

A conflict between tendencies toward making different responses, produced by desires and views, which cannot be made at the same time, implies frustration, or the blocking of goals. A decision is required by the person to determine whether he will follow the dictates of one desire or of another, or the counsel of one view or another. The tendencies toward making the many different responses compete for the limited space in the final common path to those specific effector organs which win out as the ones to produce the ultimate response.

A conflict in a child may arise when two parents set different goals for his behavior, because the child may have desires to follow the suggestions of each parent. When each parent insists stubbornly that the child follow his suggestions, the child is faced with an insoluble problem, leading ultimately to severe frustration. A similar situation would occur in industry when a supervisor gives instructions to the worker that conflict with the instructions given by the foreman. The resulting frustration is accompanied by an increase in arousal, which probably will be counterproductive for personal growth and peace of mind.

The conflicting tendencies for performing different acts can come from desires, views, or combinations of these. An example of conflicting views would be the case of a person from a different ethnic background from his neighbors. The standards for his particular minority group may conflict with the standards of the larger society. The person is torn between his desires to conform to both standards. Often this conflict is reduced to the problem of deciding between what his parents propose and what his friends advise, or, later in life, between what he learned as a child and what his present life situation seems to dictate.

Another illustration of such conflicting views is when a parent states verbally one set of standards for the child but by his own actions sets a different standard for imitation. The child is in a conflict between the two views of proper behavior proposed by the parent. The conflicting demands of "don't do as I do, but do as I say" naturally are confusing, as I pointed out before.

Approach-Avoidance

When the attainment of satisfaction for a desire is blocked in some manner, the consequent increase of arousal beyond a reasonable limit is unpleasant to the person. Under high arousal an act may be done which is very inappropriate to the particular input or to the situation in general. In this case, it would be an act that is habitual or characteristic of that person. For example, if a man is accustomed to yelling at his wife or beating the dog, he is likely to do either one or both if he is highly aroused by some conflict. Such acts are particularly probable if it is not possible to make the appropriate response which would otherwise be given in that situation. Such a circumstance could arise if a person had a job which required dealing with the public. He might be provoked by a customer, for example, but prevented from expressing his ire by usual company policy against "punching out" customers. The helpmate or Fido might suffer the consequences.

In the above example the attainment of the goal—to punch the offending customer—is blocked by a conflicting desire of the employee—the desire to keep his job. He therefore experiences what psychologists call an "approach-avoidance conflict." The "approach" means that he wants to approach the goal, which is to release his anger by the act of punching the customer. The "avoidance" means that he wants to avoid losing his job, which would happen if he did perform that act. Punching out his wife at home could be a substitute goal, which would provide some satisfaction, although probably not as much as punching the customer. On the other hand, he probably would not be as likely to lose his job for wife-beating as for punching customers.

The man described above is still in a conflict at home, of course, because he has reason to avoid punching out his wife. Whether or not he does commit this low act depends upon his assessment of the "payoff."

The amount of satisfaction he gets depends upon how much his wife reminds him of the customer. The avoidance tendency is determined by such things as his calculation of the odds that his wife will leave him if he punches her out, how sorry he will be to see her go, and whether or not he really dislikes hurting her anyway. If the cost of punching his wife is too great, there is still Fido.

Of course, there are good reasons for not beating up on Fido. One of them is that he could run into trouble with the law for mistreating animals. Also, he might lose his best friend.

Approach-Approach

Another source of frustration is an approach-approach conflict. These conflicts create smaller problems because here the person is torn between two attractive goals, both of which he desires. His only problem is that he cannot have them both. For example, he cannot spend the same vacation days in the mountains and at the seashore. He cannot both save his money and spend it on a good time. The teenager cannot eat all of the goodies he likes and still have a clear complexion and slim body to attract members of the opposite sex.

This type of conflict does not last long. Usually, once the person takes the first step toward one goal, the pull toward that goal grows in value. The attractiveness of the other goal correspondingly diminishes, because it is psychologically more remote.

Avoidance-Avoidance

A third general type of conflict is "avoidance-avoidance." Here the problem for the person is to choose the "lesser of two evils." His preferred act is, naturally, to "leave the field," if he can. To leave the field is to get out of the situation so that neither alternative act must be made. Probably the best example of this would be that of a young male who is opposed to war and faces a military draft. He does not want to serve in the military, nor does he want to go to jail for evading the draft. One possible resolution to this conflict is to leave the field—to go to a foreign nation which will grant him asylum. Often there are external barriers which prevent the person from leaving the field. This results in a very persistent conflict.

Once the person takes a step toward one undesired outcome, it grows in strength, becomes even more objectionable. Therefore, the person reverses his direction, and moves toward the other act. The second alternative now becomes more undesirable, with the desire to avoid the first one diminished in strength. This process may continue, with the person oscillating back and forth between the two acts, neither of which he wants to do. He finally will stop responding at all, unable to choose either alternative. His ability to adjust will then be small indeed, while the unpleasant feelings of arousal will persist.

Double Approach-Avoidance

In the case of human beings in complex situations, the alternative choices are so numerous, and the motivations so varied, that conflict situations often have many approach and many avoidance aspects. One course of action may involve both desired and undesired consequences. Another, incompatible, action also may involve both positive and negative aspects. Leaving the field may be possible but undesirable for some reason. Reaching a decision under these circumstances is even more difficult than in the simpler situations. Psychologists then refer to double approach-avoidance conflicts. In the last analysis, the person will take the path that he anticipates will cause him at that moment the most pleasure or the least displeasure.

Frustration

High levels of arousal in a person present the danger that the person is more likely to perform some act—any act—regardless of how the arousal was produced. The force to propel the act is there, and almost any stimulus, weak or strong, can set it off. The person is like a powder keg, or a steam kettle, waiting to explode. We sometimes say, "He's an accident looking for a place to happen." The resultant act may be displaced toward an inappropriate goal, or it may be an appropriate one that he is set or strongly prepared to do, but which is in response to the wrong signal. For example, the sprinter may "jump the gun" out of the starting blocks because someone coughs or explodes a paper bag in the stands.

The response of a person to frustration is thus like the changed path of a river when it is blocked by an obstruction. It will try to push aside the blockage or make a new riverbed to find a new outlet; it will take the path of least resistance. In the case of a person, the act which becomes the outlet will depend upon the weaknesses and strengths of the person.

Reactions to Frustration

Different persons will select different ways of draining off the excess arousal. The following is a description of a few responses to frustration.

The substitution of a different response, or "displacement," has been mentioned as a reaction to frustration. The similarity of the response determines the effectiveness of this method.

Other responses, or combinations of responses, to frustration are also frequent, depending upon the person. One of these is "aggression," attacking another person or group of persons. The simplest form of aggression is to overpower a person who possesses a desired object and will not give it up or share it. The frustrated person merely takes what he wants, aggressively, or performs hostile acts against the person who he perceives as responsible for his frustration. An example of this is the rage of inner-city blacks, who are largely blocked from economic, social, and other goals and who may, therefore, heed the cry, "Burn, baby, burn." One has to explore deeply the characteristics of some inner-city blacks to be able to understand why they turn away from aggression toward substitution of beneficial responses and follow the cry, "Build, baby, build."

Another response to frustration is "fixation." This means that the person latches onto some act and performs it over and over again when he is in a particular situation. Because there are usually more wrong acts than right ones possible in a problem situation, he is more likely to select a nonadjustive or ineffective act. The person may continue to perform that act even though he knows that it is not helping to solve his conflict. He may go fishing—leaving the field—when the problem arises. He may perform some aggressive act. He may become sexually promiscuous. He may possibly turn to the bottle and become an alcoholic.

Another frequent response to frustration is "denial," in which the person denies that he has a problem. This reaction is not adaptive, of course, because one is not likely to solve a problem which he thinks does not exist. Nevertheless, the problem and the frustration do exist, and the frustration may lead to some other act, which in all probability will not be effective in resolving the conflict. Often, the response of "rationalization" accompanies that of denial. The person makes up a plausible story to tell himself and others which explains why he has no problem. He might say, for example, that he did not really desire the unobtainable goal. This is the well known "sour-grapes" situation. In the extreme case, the person may even convince himself that he wants exactly the opposite of his true desires. An example of this might be the rejected suitor who decides that he hates, not loves, the girl.

"Regression" is another frequent reaction to frustration. The person uses again old acts which were appropriate and useful to him at a previous stage of his development. An example of this would be the child who has been toilet-trained but suddenly loses control when a new baby is brought home from the hospital. The act of messing his pants got him attention from mother before, and he wants her attention now, particularly because he must share it with baby sister. Adults also show regressive behavior; consider the boss who flies into a temper tantrum when things are not progressing well with his workers.

The most adjustive response to frustration is "reorganization" of the way one thinks about the situation. One such response would be to give up an unattainable goal and to set a new, more realistic one. Or, by looking at the old problem in a new way, the person might discover a way of solving it. In either of these cases, the old problem is resolved by reasoning or insight.

Serious unresolved conflicts may lead to a stalled decision process, much like a machine jammed by conflicting instructions. Consider again an example using the automobile, as in chapter 5. The reasonable driver does not step on the accelerator to cause the automobile to surge ahead and then immediately throw the gear selector into reverse. If he did, the machine would probably become at least temporarily unable to function and perhaps permanently damaged. This result is like mental illness in a person. Conflicting signals or codes motivate him to do different things, so that his capacity to decide rationally becomes damaged, at least temporarily.

Frustration Tolerance

The above discussion was not meant to imply that frustration is always bad and that one should always attempt to eliminate or prevent it. Actually, it is not possible to eliminate all frustration; no one can always get what he wants when he wants it. Therefore, a person must learn to cope with some frustration.

A child should experience small amounts of frustration as he grows so that he can develop some tolerance for it. In this way, he will be able to work out ways of adjusting to frustrating events instead of resorting to nonadjustive and antisocial acts. As he matures and therefore develops more tolerance for frustration, the amounts that he can be asked to endure can be increased. The mature adult has a substantial amount of tolerance for frustration and, therefore, is less strongly aroused by it. Consequently, he is better able to make the necessary adaptive responses.

Stress of Decisions

Making a decision requires some arousal in the person. The constant necessity for making decisions would therefore eventually lead to the desire to reduce this arousal. The most familiar example of this is the business executive who is likely to develop stomach ulcers, reflecting the effects of such stressful levels of arousal. A famous experiment done by J. V. Brady in 1958 clarifies the process by which the ulcer may be developed. Brady used monkeys in his study because of the obvious disadvantages of using human subjects. He placed pairs of monkeys in restraining chairs, and arranged to deliver noxious electric shocks to them at regular intervals. One monkey, the "executive," could turn off the shock for both animals by pushing a lever. This executive monkey usually developed stomach ulcers. The other monkey, who in fact received the same number of shocks as the executive, did not develop ulcers. Therefore, the responsibility for making the decisions produced greater effects of stress than just the noxious experience.

Nonresponses

The important aspect of the decision process is that the final payoff, the overt act, results from it. Thus, a person may have an inclination to do one thing, but as a result of other considerations does something else. Good intentions are not very beneficial if they do not produce good acts.

Unfortunately, there are many situations in which time limitations require a quick response. If the person has too much of an internal conflict, so that he wavers between possible responses or is frozen into inactivity, then he may not be able to make an adaptive response in time. The withholding of a response, or a failure to take one of the alternative adjustive actions, is also a response. This response is not likely to be adaptive, however. It may allow the frustration-producing conflict to continue indefinitely.

Summary

This chapter discusses the processes by which a person selects which acts he will perform in a given situation. The choice of act is a result of the tendencies toward certain responses produced by the desires and the views.

The decision processes may be unknown to the person or he may be consciously aware of them. They may be automatic and reflexive, or prolonged and reflective. Experience was held out as the key to rational decisions, which occur when the views exert a greater effect than the desires in determining which act is chosen. Experience comes with age, of course, but this effect is increased by good educational environments. The tendencies toward producing responses may both facilitate the production of the same response, or they may conflict by facilitating competing responses.

Conflicts between different views and desires mean that the person is blocked from the satisfaction of making some desired responses or becomes frustrated. Reactions to frustration include substitution, denial, regression, and reorganization. Building up a tolerance for frustration is necessary because some frustration is inevitable. When the conflicting views produce about equal tendencies to make incompatible responses, the person may be able to make neither response. This resultant failure to act—which is itself an act—is not likely to be adjustive.

9. Behavior

Acts are meaningful units of behavior. Some may be easily observed, as with normal speech or large movements of the limbs. Other acts are so small that they are hidden from the unaided eye. These can be small muscle twitches, responses of internal organs, or even neural responses within the brain itself.

The responses of internal organs include changes in the rate of heartbeats, increased or decreased stomach contractions, secretions from certain glands, and so forth, which are frequently associated with emotional reactions. For example, the so-called "lie detector" machine measures the changed electrical conductivity of the skin when the individual is emotionally aroused, based on the assumption that most persons exhibit the physiological response associated with the subjective emotion when telling a lie. A person who did not become emotionally aroused by telling a lie would therefore not be caught by this device. Conversely, an innocent person might well give an emotional response because he is upset that he is involved in a criminal investigation. Thus, the observed response gives us a clue to the nature of the inner psychological processes, but it does not tell us simply, directly and infallibly the content of these processes.

Availability of Acts

The selection of which act to perform in some particular situation is dependent upon the total array of acts that are available to the person. Some limitation on the number of possible acts is placed by existing conditions. For example, it is usually not possible after a football game in a crowded stadium just to walk normally to the exit; the press of people forces a much slower pace than one usually prefers. Another example is the selection of what to eat for dinner at a restaurant; the diner is limited to the choices on the menu.

Limitations on the possible acts can also be placed by characteristics of the person himself. No matter how much I may wish to, I cannot entertain at a party by playing a banjo, for the simple reason that I cannot play the banjo. Other responses I could make, however, if I were able to overcome certain internal barriers which ordinarily block their execution. For example, I might sing a solo at the party if I could overcome my shyness, assuming also the hostess' forbearance.

Thus, in any given stimulus situation, some acts are more likely to be given than others. This may be because of the built-in reflexes, or it may be caused by the habits which the person has formed from past experiences. If for some reason these highly available habits cannot be given, or the person is not rewarded for giving them, other responses which were previously less available will then be made. The acts which are not likely to be given initially in a particular situation, are for that reason much more difficult for the person to learn, because the person must first learn not to give the responses for which initially he had stronger tendencies, and then learn to make the other less likely responses.

Sometimes a given act has been so successful previously in solving a person's adjustment problems that the learning has been too strong. Then, if that act is not successful later in some new situations, the individual has few other acts that are easily available to him. He continues making the act which is still highly available, carrying it over into situations where it may not be effective. For example, the authoritarian approach in his relations to people may work well for him at his office, school, or plant, but not at all well at lodge meetings. Therefore, the successful businessman may not become a successful member of the lodge.

As mentioned in the last chapter, in extreme cases the behavior can be abnormally "fixated" due to frustration. When a person has been continually frustrated by failure to solve a problem, sometimes he settles upon one act which he blindly and rigidly makes even though it does not promote a helpful response. Because this act is not acquired by learning, it is difficult to eliminate; the person never makes a different response which can be rewarded or shaped. In such a case, maximum guidance or direction is necessary; the person must be prevented in some manner from making the fixated response and somehow forced into making the appropriate response, which can then be rewarded. Professional help is clearly indicated in such cases.

Setting Goals

Before effective guidance can begin, the subject and guide must define what behaviors are desired. As one psychologist mentioned with respect to a psychotherapist giving guidance to a client, "One of you in the room needs to know where you are going." This is important because once the goals are established, it becomes necessary for all persons concerned with the guidance of that individual to work consistently toward those goals. In the case of parents, they must agree with each other on the goals that are set for the child. If they do not know what they want of the child, it is obviously confusing for the child to know which behaviors are expected of him, or how to resolve the conflict between the different standards.

The guide should set his goals for the person in terms of a broad perspective. Sometimes the would-be guide picks one act that he wants to be done by the person under his guidance and forsakes all other goals. It was my unhappy experience to encounter a school principal who apparently desired the child's conformity to school regulations above all else. He had his own version of an isolation unit for stubborn offenders, a small storeroom adjoining the main office. He would literally put a child into this unit until he "broke," and begged to be allowed the chance to be "good." The principle is the same as for the "hole" in prisons: namely, to make life conditions so unpleasant that the offender is willing to make any concession to improve them. This principal bragged to me that his method always worked, and furthermore that once he "broke" the child he never had any further behavioral problem with him. I didn't doubt it! Aside from the poor ethics of this treatment, the effects on the mental health and creativity of the victim had to be harmful.

As was pointed out in chapter 5, the parent can get the child to eat his undesired spinach if the parent is willing to starve the child until he eats it. This approach requires the parent to be firm when the child pleads for food other than spinach. The parent must decide how important it is for the child to eat spinach; he should not start anything that he is not prepared to finish. The child in all likelihood will not die of spinach deficiency. On the other hand, the parent would obviously not give the child poisoned food or a loaded gun, no matter how hard he pleaded. These decisions about what will and will not be tolerated must be made early so that they can be followed consistently. The decisions may be made on practical, ethical, psychological, or other bases.

The question that the parent, teacher, foreman, friend, or other guide must ask himself is whether or not the responses that he is permitting or prohibiting for his subject-person are for the benefit of that person or for the benefit of someone else—possibly the guide himself. The answer depends upon the general attitude of the guide toward that subject-person. As discussed in chapter 3, true concern frequently results in the denial to oneself of certain selfish emotional satisfactions.

Obviously, not everything a child wants to do, or everything the parent wants to give the child, is good for the child. The good parent denies the child such harmful things. On the other hand, the good parent permits the child to do something because it is best for him, not because the child begs to do it. For example, to permit the child to take a trip with friends or relatives without the parents may require real parental courage and selflessness. The parents understand that the child must experience increasing degrees of independence from them as he grows older, in order to be able to cope with life later on. After assuring themselves as best they can that proper safety precautions will be maintained, the good parents endure the anxiety of wondering whether someone else will actually maintain sufficient vigilance for the child's safety.

Individual Goals

The goals for guidance should be set with concern for the individual person; depending upon his capabilities, we may expect more or less from him. For example, one would not expect a child to become an accomplished artist if he had no artistic talent, nor would one expect him to become a musician if he were tone-deaf. A child who had some deficit because of brain injury should not be expected to perform in all tasks as well as an uninjured child, and so forth. In sum, the goals should be realistic with respect to the potential achievement of the particular person.

Problems in Setting Goals

Setting goals is not easy. Very often, the decision about what are the proper acts for a person involves moral issues and value judgments. Although these issues are outside the field of psychology, in such areas as religion, economics, and philosophy, nevertheless, they are necessary for the implementation of a sound, practical psychology.

In order to set reasonable goals for the individual person, one must learn more about him, understand what his capabilities and limitations are. The guide needs to know the subject's level of readiness to move on to a new stage of development, so that all proposed goals are reasonably attainable.

As was mentioned in the first chapter of this book, we can always cite principles for guidance which seem to conflict with one another. Many acts represent acceptable personal adjustments up to some limit but are harmful if carried to excess. As an example, consider the proper degree of conformity. Obviously, some conformity is necessary; a person failing to conform at all is very likely to land either in jail or in a mental institution. He can wear bizarre clothes down Main Street, but if he carries the nonconformity to the extreme of wearing no clothes at all, he is likely to have problems with the authorities.

I often ask the students in my classes whether or not they think that a person should be guided toward becoming more conformist. The discussion is lively, with many arguments on both sides, until someone points out that I have asked an unanswerable question. The proper answer is: "It all depends." It depends on the degree of conformity presently shown by the subject-person. If he is already too different from the persons with whom he is trying to interact, he would probably function within that society more effectively if he conformed more. Another person may be so concerned with conforming, however, that he throttles his own potential for creative living. He might drown his own individual desires and views in a blind attempt to imitate the actions and follow the dictates of others.

Another issue is the degree of permissiveness in expression which should be permitted. Some permissiveness enables the person to reduce tension, reducing the chances of frustration because goals are not blocked. However, as we have discussed before, a certain amount of frustration is necessary for the development of persistence of purpose, self-discipline, and frustration tolerance. Also, self-confidence is generated by experience in coping with frustrating problems, just as the soles of the feet are toughened by walking over rocky ground.

All parties should know, however, which acts will be permitted and which not. There should be a tolerance for differences in behavior of the exceptional person. Each person can be more effective if he is allowed to "do his thing." The guide should nevertheless establish limits for the behavior within which negotiation can take place. Otherwise the person being guided might feel betrayed if he is limited in an area in which he was led to believe that he could make his own decision. Obviously, the limits must prevent him from doing anything that is too dangerous, immoral, or illegal. Such acts are not as easily defined as one might expect. For example, the issue of illegal acts and the problem of civil disobedience present a conflict of two codes of behavior. Other moral questions can similarly present many conflicting alternatives.

The general goal of the parent and the educator is to prepare a person for learning and training experiences, so that he will be able to adjust to, or cope with, whatever problems he will probably encounter in the future. Desirable acts assist the child in actualizing his potential so that he can be happy and can make his best contribution to society. Obviously, different people will be able to make different contributions.

In setting the standards of behavior for a child, very often adults expect more of the youth than they do of themselves. Some years ago, when my son played baseball on a league for preteenage youths, the coaches often required the kids to run laps around the field for protesting a decision by the umpire. Sometimes immediately thereafter, the coaches themselves would make far stronger complaints. Nevertheless, I never observed any of them running laps for arguing with the umpires. Apparently only the kids needed exercise in building character. The inconsistency and unfairness of these behaviors never seemed to occur to these coaches. But their message was clear: "Don't do as I do, do as I say." How could the kids know which behavior was correct?

My wife observed another example of such behavior on the part of so-called adults at a teacher's meeting. She had the misfortune to sit in front of three teachers who talked to one another throughout the entire meeting, disturbing everyone around them. Undoubtedly, these same teachers would never tolerate such talking by members of their classes while they themselves were teaching. Again, this is evidence for the setting of higher standards of conduct for the children than the adults are willing to set for themselves. It is small wonder that our youth often charge older members of the establishment with hypocrisy.

Thus, one of the major problems in setting desired acts for youths is the conflict between the goals and status of the youngster and those of the adult. Our society does not have puberty rites which signal that the youth has become an adult and is therefore entitled to the rights and responsibilities of the adult. We therefore treat the adolescent at times as a child and at other times as an adult. Because we set too many conflicting goals for the children of our society, the adolescents are in constant conflict about which standards to adopt for themselves. An experience from my own youth illustrates this. During World War II, I volunteered at the age of seventeen for military service. Presumably I was mature enough for this adult task. On the way home, however, I was refused the opportunity to rent a rowboat, because I was too young to be trusted with one. Nevertheless, a very short time later I was a qualified helmsman on an aircraft carrier.

Short- and Long-Term Goals

If nothing short of complete attainment of long-term goals is expected, and the person does not soon achieve one of these goals, he has the disadvantage of experiencing failure rather than success. Therefore short-term, as well as long-term, goals of behavior are necessary, because the appropriate reward for achieving the short-term goal can be obtained relatively soon. Each person should be able to achieve some goals, and therefore receive some rewards quickly, before he gives up entirely. Each short-term goal should be a step toward a major long-term goal. This is an obvious matter of efficiency.

The relative values of the different goals should be kept in mind. For example, if parents take a permissive point of view, and let the child have increased independence, the child will in fact develop greater independence—if he lives. The parent always has to balance this possible gain in the development of independence with the possible danger to the child of such independence. In some areas of behavior, it is tolerable for the child to make mistakes. If he overwaters a plant and it dies, he can learn by the experience. If, however, he makes a mistake on his bicycle and is killed on the highway, he has no chance to learn better.

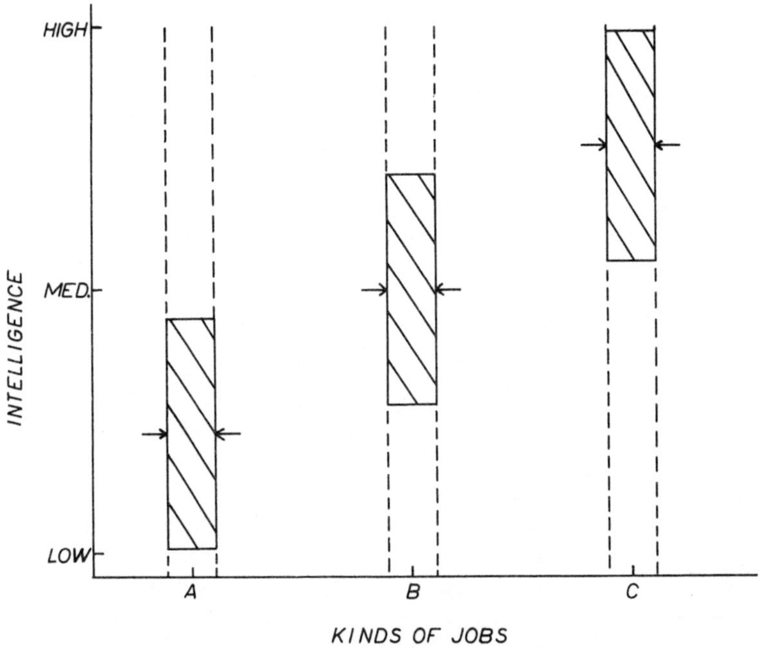

Figure 9-1. Illustration of the variability of levels of intelligence within different kinds of jobs.

In setting long-term goals, like the selection of a vocation, both the skills and interests of the person must be considered. High motivation to succeed in a job can to some extent overcome a lack of natural ability. The situation is described schematically in figure 9-1. The horizontal dimension represents three kinds of jobs, and the vertical dimension represents varying degrees of intelligence. The striped boxes indicate the typical ranges of intelligence shown by most people who are successful in each job, with the little arrows representing the average intelligence of people in that job. Although Job C seems to require a higher level of intellectual ability than Job A and Job B, and B more than A, the range of extreme scores overlaps. Obviously there are some persons in Job B who are more intelligent than some persons working in Job C, and some in Job A more intelligent than some in Job B. Thus other factors, such as motivation to succeed and emotional stability, are involved in success on these jobs. These other factors should be taken into account when predicting the future success of a person.

Clearly, however, the person with a lowest level of intelligence would probably not succeed in Job C, and should not be advised to attempt that job.

Evaluating Acts

In many ways, it is difficult to evaluate the success of the guide in directing behavior. In the case of a parent, the yardstick of success is to have a generally successful, healthy, and happy offspring who has grown to maturity. Specific yardsticks for success might be the amount of money earned or the social prestige within the community. There are more formal types of achievement tests or measures of success, which have the value of informing both the person and the guide of the degree of success. The achievement test tells us what the person has been able to accomplish as a result of both his native intelligence and the motivation with which he applied himself to learning and performing the task.

Any test reflects the performance, or acts, of an individual under a given set of circumstances. The various criteria of a good test were previously discussed in chapter 4. For the testing procedure to be valid, it must assume that the person is performing to the best of his ability, that emotional or other interfering problems are not controlling his acts. A person may very well perform at a level far below his general level of capability unless an effort is made to get him to perform at his best.

Frequently, assessments of acts are used to predict future behavior of an individual on the basis of such relationships as shown in figure 9-1. These tests are, however, much more useful for predicting average performance of a group than for predicting the performance of an individual person. The psychological literature is filled with cases of persons who scored very poorly on aptitude tests, but subsequently became highly successful, contrary to very confident prediction. For example, one of my college students scored so poorly on a verbal aptitude test that one would not have expected him even to graduate from college. But this same person eventually became a highly successful graduate student and, later, a college professor.

Many people have used evidence such as the foregoing to conclude that we should not use psychological tests. The correct solution is, however, not to do away with the psychological tests, but to increase the training and skill of the consumer in the use and interpretation of test results. It is not the fault of the test if a personnel officer decides to use cut-off scores in a rigid, mindless way.

The problem exists in assessing the adequacy of the testing task for tapping what the person has learned, and can do. For example, a person may have learned well the content of the course in school, enough to do well on the final examination, but he may also have learned hostile attitudes toward the schoolteacher, or toward the material itself, which do not show up directly on the written examination.

In setting the goals for a person, we should not give him verbal instructions as to what sort of behavior we want, then evaluate his performance on some other basis. One of my children had a schoolteacher who asked the students in his class to jot down in a notebook each day their thoughts about life. In the first place, to my mind, this is an invasion of privacy. The stated purpose of the notebook was to encourage each child to think deeply and broadly about life and about where and how the course material could fit into this philosophy. Unfortunately, the whole situation was further compounded at examination time, when this same teacher tested the students on rote memorization of the facts and dates in the assigned textbook. The students were learning simultaneously to mistrust the verbal guidance of the teacher, to expect punishment (namely, a low grade) for thinking seriously about the material of the course and relating it to personal needs and views, and to be rewarded for memorization by rote.

Mental Health

Although mental health is generally sought as a goal, it is extremely difficult to define. It may be generally defined as a stable state in a person who is well-adjusted, enjoys life, and who is attaining actualization of his personal potential. It is a positive state and not merely an absence of symptoms of illness.

The distinction between the normal healthy state and the abnormal state is not clear-cut; the one blends into the other. The same person could show, at one time, normal behavior and, at another time, abnormal behavior. When touring a mental hospital, it is not always easy to detect which are the patients and which are the attendants or psychiatrists. As a matter of fact, in my student days, one member of my class was visiting the hospital and was inadvertently locked in. He was unable to convince the attendants that he was just visiting, because they were accustomed to patients saying that they did not belong in the hospital, but were only visiting to study hospital conditions. The student finally had to call the chairman of the psychology department to verify his identity.

Some behaviors seem unusual and therefore indicative of abnormal personality unless one understands the reason for the behavior. A story is told in one school system of a young child who used only the dark purple water colors in his art class. The teachers and principal were rather concerned about this behavior because they felt that it indicated a dark and gloomy outlook on life. Finally, the school psychologist asked the child why he was using only this paint; he replied that it was the only can of paint the other kids had not spit in.

There are permissible degrees of deviation from average kinds of behaviors that can be shown by a person without meaning that he is abnormal. For example, an examination of the normal curve in chapter 2 (figure 2-2) shown no clear-cut dividing lines between the acts that are normal—that is, near the center of the distribution—and those that are abnormal—towards the ends of the distribution. The only acts that are of real concern are those that are at the extreme edges. These are literally the "far-out" responses.

It is important for the guide to learn to recognize the acts that indicate abnormal tendencies in the personality. These acts are different from the normal in either direction, either much above or far below the average, or norm. For example, the kids who act out their emotional problems can show abnormal behavior, but the very quiet, unhappy and withdrawn children also can represent potential problems of adjustment.

It is important to recognize the normal causes of mental illness. Mental illness is not some supernatural state akin to the possession of the person by devils. Although the question of whether mental illness is inherited or caused by experience has not been answered to date, certainly experience typically contributes to it. Mentally ill parents tend to have mentally ill children, probably because the parents give the children most of their environmental experiences, as well as their inherited structure. Because parents are in contact with the children far more frequently and for longer periods than anyone else, it is very difficult for a school or other governmental agency to combat a poor home environment in just the relatively few hours a day that they have the children under their guidance.

Summary

There are various types or levels of acts, including covert, internal emotional reactions as well as gross motor movements. The concept of levels of availability for different acts in a situation means that the person is more likely to perform some acts than others in certain situations. The function of rewards is to move the more desired acts from lower in the order of availability up to more favorable positions.

The major problems of establishing the desirability of different acts were described as primarily moral and philosophical issues, although certain psychological criteria are relevant. A broad perspective in evaluating the relative desirability of acts is necessary. Methods for evaluating the obtained acts against the goals involve the use of tests. Achievement of short-term minor goals should not prevent the attainment of longer, more critical goals. The acts which indicate mental health should be considered to be more quantitatively than qualitatively different from those that indicate pathology.

10. Reward and Punishment

The guide can change the likelihood for repetition of a desired act by the way he rewards the act when it appears. Any act followed by a positive (desired) reward will have an increased probability for repetition; any act not followed by a desired reward, or by a negative event (punishment) will decrease in probability.

A change in the previous behavior indicates, of course, that learning has occurred. Learning is defined as a relatively persistent change in behavior caused by experience in the learning situation. Thus, learning is not observed directly, but inferred from the change in behavior. This distinction between the actual performance and learning as a change in performance reflects the fact that many things other than learning can control the behavior, as we have previously discussed. For example, performance can be affected by maturation and by changes in motivation.

If an increase in the strength of an act is desired, then obviously that act should be followed by a positive reward in the proper situation. A positive reward is a condition that satisfies some desire of the person. Therefore, the rewards are selected in terms of prevailing motivations; different rewards have different degrees of effectiveness, depending upon the desires of the individuals. This is the topic of incentives, as discussed in chapter 7.

To the extent that persons have similar motivations, then similar events can be rewarding to them. Therefore, some events commonly are rewarding, although some persons do not respond to rewards normal for most people. Some authors have even suggested that mental illness is nothing other than the failure of the person to respond to the usual rewards.

If the act is not desired by the guide, then he must never reward it. Under some circumstances, it may even be necessary for him to use punishment, which is establishing a condition not desired by the person. Such punishment may be necessary if the act performed by the person is dangerous to himself or to others. Punishment may also have to be used as a "stopper" to weaken a very strong habitual response sufficiently to allow the proper response when reward has not been possible because the proper act has not appeared to have been rewarded.

The person does not have to be aware that a response is being rewarded for him to learn it; therefore, he can be taught a response without his knowledge or conscious cooperation. Similarly, the guide may not be aware that he is rewarding a response and therefore causing his subject-person to learn it. Consequently, two people can even be guiding each other to new responses of which neither is aware, and of which neither would approve if he were making a conscious choice.

Reward is effective even if the act was not itself successful in the achievement of the reward. If the act is learned, but it was not instrumental in producing the reward, we attribute the behavior to a superstition. A striking demonstration of such superstitious behavior was provided by B. F. Skinner (1948). Skinner arranged for a clock-controlled apparatus to deliver food to the cage of each of several pigeons at regular intervals, regardless of what the bird was doing. Typically, each animal began to learn some idiosyncratic response. The acquired response was different for the different birds because it depended upon the particular behavior of the individual bird at the moment the food happened to arrive. Whatever the behavior—turning around in the cage clockwise, thrusting the head into one corner of the cage, pecking toward the floor—it was more likely to be occurring later, having been followed by reward, when the next reward happened along.

The practical implications of the Skinner study are enormous. Because the rewards establish responses with which they are associated, even though the connection is only accidental, guides should therefore avoid coincidentally rewarding a person who has performed an undesired act. The unintentional, coincidental reward can be as effective in stamping in the undesired behavior as if it had been given deliberately.

The learned acts may be simple habits, such as tugging on the ear lobe, clearing the throat, or putting on the left shoe first. They may, however, be more complex, such as those required in the performance of motor skills like woodcarving, surgery, typing, and singing an aria. Learned behavior would also include the performance of very complex social behaviors, such as the proper method for removing a seed from the mouth at a formal dinner, for convincing a friend to run for an office in the club, or for "telling off" an obnoxious neighbor. Also, as discussed in chapter 7, the responses can include the development of specific meanings for words and signs, and the acquisition of attitudes and opinions.

Learning may be oriented toward education or toward training. Training is pointed toward the acquisition of certain acts which are known to be important in an anticipated situation. The person would be trained to do a certain job, such as medicine or automobile repair, for example. Education, on the other hand, is aimed at increasing the variety of available acts for a variety of situations, many of which cannot be anticipated. The appropriate acts can then be applied to the practical situations as they arise. Training a person is easier because the guide knows generally what situations are likely to be encountered and what acts are appropriate in that situation. In contrast, education—or in a large sense, personality development—aims to increase adjustive or problem-solving ability so that the person can act appropriately in any situation which he encounters.

Kinds of Learning Situations

Several different kinds of learning situations can be distinguished. These different types may be occurring at the same time.

Trial and Error

The first type of learning is the familiar "trial and error" situation, in which the person attempts to solve a problem by making some responses that he thinks might work. Unsuccessful responses are replaced by different ones. The individual keeps making different responses until one produces a desired outcome. He is rewarded either by the intrinsic satisfaction of having achieved the correct response, or by some extrinsic device, such as the reception of money, food, or praise. Therefore, the next time he is in that situation, he is likely to make the rewarded response earlier, thus receiving the reward earlier. After a number of such trials, he will promptly make the correct act and be rewarded.

If the person cannot make a good guess about what act is likely to produce the reward, he must make a variety of different responses, selected at random. Unless the desired act is just to lie still and relax, the person will not solve the problem unless he keeps responding actively. Sometimes—in cases of overwork, for example—the desired act is just that—to relax and become inactive. Often, however, the desired behavior requires the active responding. Therefore, the person who is more active and tries more different acts in the situation is the one who will hit upon the correct act sooner, thus learning sooner. Of course, within limits, the level of activity can be increased by increasing the motivation of the learner, improving his chances for learning.

One important factor in education is to teach the person to keep trying different acts until he reaches a solution, because the person who stays "in a rut," continually trying the same incorrect, unrewarded act, will be greatly hindered in his attempts at learning. I have several times failed to solve a problem until I broke out of a rut in my thinking by trying something that I was sure would not lead to the solution. This forced me to see the problem from a different angle, and ultimately led to the solution.

Stimulus Substitution

Another kind of learning involves the substitution of stimuli. In this learning situation, two unrelated stimuli are presented together for a number of trials. After a number of such pairings, the response which is ordinarily given to one of the stimuli appears in response to the other stimulus as well. While the response is appropriate—given naturally—to the original stimulus, it is not necessarily appropriate to the other member of the pair, which nevertheless has gained the ability to evoke it. This type of learning was discovered by Russian physiologist I. P. Pavlov (1927). After Pavlov paired the sound of a bell and the application of meat powder to the tongue of a dog a number of times, the dog salivated to the sound of the bell, as well as to the meat powder on his tongue. That is, eventually the bell acquired the ability to produce the salivation by itself.

Thus any stimulus present when a reward is given may itself come to have rewarding properties. For example, some environments, such as a home town, have been associated with many rewards over the years. Therefore, being home for the holidays produces pleasure in itself. This can work the other way also, in the case of unpleasant experiences. A person probably would not enjoy a homecoming trip to a ghetto where he had more unpleasant than pleasant experiences.

This principle of substitution also includes reactions to another person as a stimulus. You like to be around someone who has rewarded you or has been with you during times of reward. Similarly, you do not like to be around someone who has been associated with unpleasant experiences and punishments. The moral of this is that people will like you if you give them rewards, but dislike you if you habitually give them punishments or are generally unpleasant to be around.

Perceptual

The third type of learning is perceptual learning. In this situation, the person develops the ability to discriminate among different stimuli. This occurs when the different stimuli become associated with different feedback conditions. The baby learns, for example, to tell the difference between the visual image of a bottle of milk and a can of baby powder, because sucking on each leads to different consequences. Later he learns to discriminate between red and green traffic lights, between a fiery red coal and an apple, and so forth.

This perceptual learning is particularly important because it provides a basis for future learning. The person is able to transfer the learned discriminatory capacity to new learning situations. As discussed in chapter 7, the person who has had the broad experiences to develop many discriminations will have a richer coding system to give more meaning to various stimulus inputs.

Insight

The fourth type of learning is called insight. This learning represents a rapid reorganization of the components for a solution to a problem so that the solution is reached immediately. It is characterized by a leap to perfect performance, after which the person never again makes a mistake on that problem. This may not occur, however, until many trials of slow progress have been made.

Insight does, however, depend upon prior experience with all the components of the solution which were reorganized to produce that correct solution. The moral of this is that such rapid solutions to problems are only possible for persons who have built up the proper background of experience for the insights to occur.

Reward

Rewards have the advantage of telling the individual that his act is the correct one as far as the person administering the reward is concerned. Because the reward gives satisfaction, a pleasant atmosphere is generated.

Another advantage of using rewards for desired behavior is that, before a reward is given, the person must show the correct behavior on his own, without being forced. Therefore, the reward in a sense follows an exercise of free will. If rewards are used exclusively, the person is in that sense never forced to do anything "against his will." This conception may appeal to those who have moral reservations about influencing the actions of another.

Anything that satisfies a desire of the person can serve as a reward. Examples of rewards may be smiles, gold stars, blue ribbons, preferred jobs, extra privileges and games, verbal praise, refreshments, caresses, money, grades, promotions in jobs, plaques, certificates of appreciation, and so forth. As pointed out previously, different things work best for different people.

Punishment

Punishment can tell the person that his act was not desired by the guide. Because ordinarily there are many more wrong acts to be made in a situation than correct ones, however, punishment has limited effectiveness. It does not provide information about which act is desired, except through a slow process of eliminating possibilities.

Also, the punished act may be part of a series of acts in a given practical situation, many of which are actually desirable. The punishment might not be sufficiently tied informationally to the undesired act, so that the punished person cannot tell which act is in fact being punished. Therefore, he may actually discontinue performance of a desired act. This point was illustrated beautifully by a story R. Vance Hall of the University of Kansas told at a meeting of the Virginia Psychological Association. Hall told of visiting the home of a fellow psychologist and learning that his friend was concerned because his children had picked up the habit of swearing from some new kids on the street. Rewards had not worked, because there had been no inoffensive language to reward. Hall then suggested punishment for using swear words. His friend agreed; the next instance would be punished. The opportunity came at dinner when the four-year-old son asked that someone pass the "damn peas." The father gave him a good clout, which put a damper on the dinner conversation, creating a rather awkward moment. To smooth things over, Hall asked the three-year-old daughter if he could help her to any food. Her reply was, "I can tell you right now that I don't want any of those damn peas!"

Any event not desired by the person can be punishing. Some typical examples of punishments are frowns, check marks, verbal reproof, reports to parents or superiors, demotions, hitting, extra work, docking of pay or fines, withdrawal of privileges, shaming, withholding accustomed rewards, and so forth. As with positive rewards, different types of punishment will probably work better with different persons.

Although punishment is not a preferred way of dealing with an undesirable act, as mentioned before, at times it is necessary to help break a very bad habit and to allow the performance of a good one, which can then be rewarded. Sometimes, if the bad habit is ignored, a different response might eventually be given on some occasion, and it can be rewarded. Once positive reward has started, then the guide can continue to weaken the old habit by withholding reward, and to foster the new by giving rewards.

Another possible way of breaking a bad habit, and one which is superior to punishment, is to provide a substitute response which is incompatible with the first one. This is the idea behind the behavioral change techniques which are referred to under the heading of "behavior modification." This method works by giving the client a strong stimulus which tends to produce an incompatible response. This technique will be discussed later in this chapter.

Punishment not only gains little in the direction of positive results, but it also produces a harmful psychological atmosphere between the guide and the subject. Punishments create a state of affairs that is not desired by the person. These unpleasant feelings may well become associated with the guide through the substitution-learning process. This probably will interfere with the effectiveness of the guide in shaping the behavior of the subject-person. It is important for the person to have success experiences, which are rewarded, rather than failure experiences, which are punished. In that case, the guide is associated with pleasant emotions rather than with unpleasant ones.

Shame is bad as a punishment because it tends to decrease self-esteem. The important idea is to focus on the acts rather than on the person. Also, the use of fear is generally bad because it creates a poor climate for learning, as discussed in chapter 6. However, it is functional for eliminating some very dangerous responses. Reasonable fear of certain objects and events is healthy. The child should fear such things as hot coals, sharp objects, power tools, poisons, and freeway traffic.

Principles of Learning

Psychologists debate whether or not any learning can occur in the absence of a desire to learn. Unquestionably, however, learning will be more effective if in fact the person intends to learn. Therefore, developing the desire to learn is extremely important, as was pointed out in chapter 6.

The learning which occurs is very often specific to a given situation. Therefore, the learning should take place in the situation in which the act is expected to be reproduced, or in one as similar to it as possible. This is training as defined above. Smooth performance of a supposedly learned act may be interrupted by some gross change in the stimulus situation. For example, a child may learn to perform his speech very well in his own living room, but be unable to recall the same speech in front of a class, or on stage. As will be pointed out later in the chapter, this fact can help to eliminate an undesired act. The guide tries to keep the person away from the stimuli which are producing the undesirable acts.

The progress of learning is slow or rapid depending upon the amount of background experience the person has had with that situation, or similar ones, before entering the learning situation. The general relationship between the change in performance and the number of learning trials is shown in figure 10-1. In this graph the horizontal scale represents the number of rewarded acts, from just a few, through several, to many. The vertical scale represents the strength of the act to be learned, ranging from low, through medium, to high. The curve on the graph shows an S-shaped relationship between the number of rewarded trials and the strength of the learning. This means that if there is little background for learning—the acts have not previously been frequently rewarded or the discrimination among stimuli established—the progress is slow at first, but it increases at an ever-increasing rate from Point A to Point B on the curve. The later stage of learning is more rapid. Then, a point of diminishing returns is reached (Point B), where it becomes harder and harder to add the same strength to the act with repeated trials of learning.

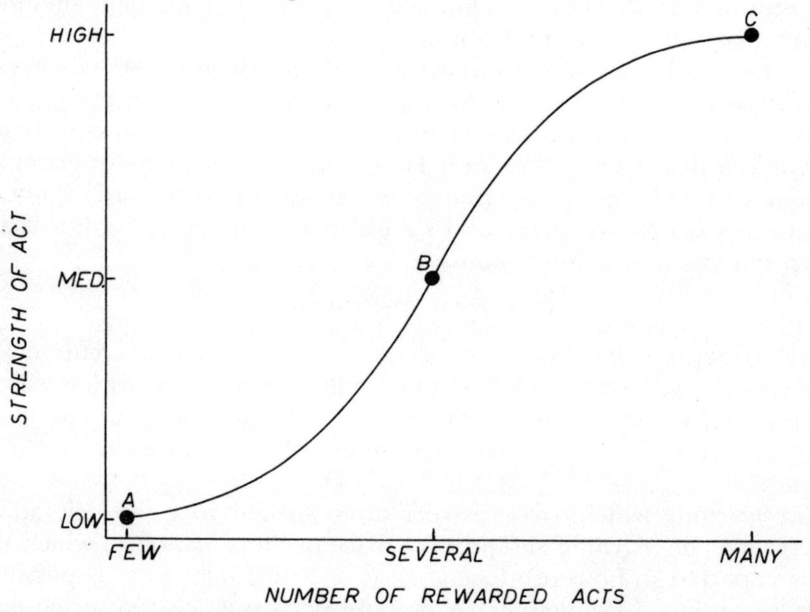

Figure 10-1. General shape of a complete learning curve showing how the strength of the act increases as the number of rewarded acts. For a given practical task only the portion of the curve from Point A to Point B, or from Point B to Point C, may be relevant.

The gains to be expected from rewarding an act would therefore depend upon where the person was in the learning process—how much background experience he had. If the person has much to learn relative to what he already knows, there will be small gains at first and then increasing gains from additional trials. In contrast, if the task components are already very well learned, the guide probably will not be able to induce the same rate of improvement with the same number of trials or rewarded acts.

Figure 10-1 shows that the rate of progress before an act is finally learned depends upon the required degree of mastery. If the guide is satisfied with a strength of the act as represented by Point B, the greatest gains are made just before the act is considered learned. On the other hand, if a high degree of mastery (near perfection) is required, as at Point C, then many, many trials of scant improvement will be necessary before that final level is achieved. It is virtually impossible to achieve sufficient strength for a very complex act that it will be performed so perfectly.

The small gains from the first several trials are characteristic of the very early stages of learning. The rapid learning that comes later builds upon this early slow learning. The person may at first be learning components of the task, or he may be learning how to go about the general task of learning. This latter learning, of general orientation and approach to the task, is what psychologists call "learning to learn." It is one vital ingredient of education, as defined earlier.

The learning curve in figure 10-1 represents a gradual (smooth) acquisition of learning. This is a "textbook" type of curve, not always manifested in reality. Some tasks would only show the segment from Points A to B, and others only that between Points B and C. Still another learner or situation may show a discontinuous curve, as in the case of insight, in which the strength of the act abruptly increases to a high level and remains there.

Also, a plateau, or flattening, in the learning curve can occur. A plateau is defined by little or no increase in performance over a number of attempts. The person may be bogged down in one approach to the task, or his desire to learn may have faltered. Often a plateau is followed by a sharp increase in learning because the person has discovered a new approach to the task, or new motivation to learn or to perform.

Schedules

Once the acts which are to be rewarded have been selected, there should be consistency in the rewards. It is bad procedure to build in a code of responding which says that one act is rewarded, if later the act is sometimes not rewarded, but punished instead. Consistency allows the person to develop trust in the guide; it gives him security. This can be overdone, however. If the consistency produces extensive rigidity in responding, the person will feel that the guide is more concerned about rules than about the welfare of the subject-person. I began to be concerned about the rigidity of regulations in the schools when my son cried out one night in his sleep, "No exceptions! No exceptions!"

Consistency has the advantage of clearly distinguishing for the person what he can do and what he cannot do. For example, neither of our children ever did anything that we decided must absolutely not be done. As a case in point, when they were toddlers we always had flowers growing in pots within their easy reach, but they never bothered a leaf. We had decided—and let the children know early—that they really must not bother the flowers. There have been a number of other things we wished they would not do, but we did not enforce these other rules with the same rigor. Therefore, we did not have as much success in controlling these other acts.

It is important not to reward bad acts, not ever. Never reward anger, aggression, or misbehavior for attention-getting, because this rewards the misconduct and will therefore increase its likelihood. Incidentally, each person should get enough attention for good behavior in order to eliminate his need to misbehave for it. Rewarding a "bad" act is harmful because of the persistent effects of partial reward. A habit which is learned through reward on some trials and not on others—one that is partially or intermittently rewarded—becomes very difficult to unlearn later. The simplest explanation for this is that the person learns he will not be rewarded every time and therefore becomes willing to tolerate the instances in which there is no reward. Going on the history of the rewards, he never knows whether or not he will get a reward the next time he performs the act, even though he has repeatedly made the act without receiving a reward.

A second reason for consistency is that the informational value of the reward and punishment is reduced if a given response is sometimes rewarded and sometimes not rewarded, or even punished. With inconsistent rewards the subject would have some understandable difficulty in knowing what the guide has in mind.

Behavior Modification

The practical rules or principles for promoting acquisition of an act can be used in programs of behavior modification, or behavioral change. Behavior modification refers to replacing abnormal or undesired acts with acts that are more beneficial. A basic procedure is, of course, to reward the desired acts and withhold rewards for the undesired acts. A formal way to set up such a program, used in mental hospitals and other institutions, is to establish what is called a "token economy." Here the person gets a reward for each desired act in the form of a token which can be exchanged for some desired object, such as candy or cigarettes, or some desired activity, such as extra privileges or furloughs. Usually the person is able to secure these incentives only by paying for them with the earned tokens.

If the main goal is to eliminate an undesired act, the basic method is to drive out the bad habit by replacing it with a good habit. Although the old habit is not likely to be lost through mere lack of use, it can probably be replaced by another act which is rewarded in its place. Ideally, the performance of the good act is incompatible with the performance of the bad act, preventing the person from performing both acts at the same time. For example, if the child is rewarded for petting the family cat, he will increase this behavior, which is obviously incompatible with the undesired behavior of pulling the cat's tail. This process is called counter-conditioning.

This mutual interference of habits can also be important in establishing a good habit, once the desired act is made on some occasions. At this point, it is particularly important to prevent a reward for a bad act under the conditions in which a good act is ordinarily rewarded.

As indicated in figure 10-1, the more times an act is rewarded, the greater the strength of the act. Therefore, repetition of the rewarded act will strengthen the habit. Sheer repetition, however, particularly without the desire of the subject to learn, and thus no reward for learning, is worse than ineffective; it can be harmful. Performing any act over and over will build up a tendency against making it again. The overly-repeated act itself becomes unpleasant, and therefore the forced repetition of it is actually punishment. This fact should be noted by teachers who have a tendency to emphasize drill and think that twenty problems of homework are always better than ten problems as a help to the pupil in understanding a particular method.

For the reward to be most effective, it should come as soon as possible after the act has been done. If the delay is too long, the reward loses its informational connection with the act and, thus, both its reward value and its informational value. The person would not understand which act earned the reward if the delay of the reward is too long.

Knowledge of results is effective by pointing out to the person which responses represented desired acts and which ones did not. Again, it is best to give the subject this knowledge as soon as possible after the act has been made.

For difficult and complicated acts which are not easily made by the person, it may be necessary to use "shaping." This approach requires rewarding successive approximations to the desired act. As the person begins to make better and better approximations to the right act, the criteria for administering the rewards change. As progress is made, the reward is withheld until an even closer approximation to the desired act is achieved. The person is led to acts that are closer and closer to the desired act until, finally, he is making the appropriate act itself. This desired behavior can then be consistently rewarded.

This shaping process requires special skills of the guide. If progress is too slow, too much reward is given for an act that is not close enough to the desired one. Then the person becomes bogged down on that act, and it is difficult to get him to move on to the next step of approximation. If, however, too much is demanded too soon, so that the person gets no rewards, he may become frustrated. Then he may become stuck on some incorrect response, or regress to an earlier form of behavior that had been rewarded previously, but which is not ultimately desired.

In general, the greater the amount of the reward, the more frequent and stronger the act. However, as has been mentioned before, the learning may be retained longer if it has been rewarded on a partial schedule. A partial schedule, as the name implies, administers rewards on only some of the trials in which the act has been correctly given. In the case of an act that one wants to establish, the time between rewards can gradually be lengthened so that the person becomes accustomed to making the correct act without expecting a reward on every trial. This is what the unions call the "stretch-out" with respect to incentive pay. As the workers increase production because of incentives, the base-rate—established on the basis of what an average, standard worker should accomplish—is renegotiated, so that incentive bonuses become harder to achieve.

Learning proceeds more rapidly if the act to be required has meaning for the individual. If he is able to fit the stimulus configuration into his own frame of reference, encode it into his own coding system, then he will be able to produce it more accurately. This is the advantage of any learning technique which requires the active participation of the learner. This is exemplified in the learning system referred to as "SQ3R" (Scan, Question, Read, Recite, Review). This approach to learning school material, for example, suggests that the person first scan the material to get an overview of its general message, the gist of the material. The second step is to question—to ask himself what are the important points covered in the material. The third step is to read the material thoroughly, with his previous questions in mind. This is followed by active recitation of it from memory, to refresh it in his mind, and to inform him of what he does not remember. The final step is to review the material periodically after it has once been learned. This last step is likely to produce what is called "overlearning." Overlearning means that the material is learned better than is just necessary to get by. As was mentioned in chapter 6, the sufficiently overlearned act can be made even under stressful conditions, such as those produced by achievement examinations.

The final hint for promoting learning is to break a very difficult task down into its component parts for learning. Then, as each part is learned, it can be added to those already learned. After all of the parts are learned individually, the learner can put them together into a whole.

Role of Guide

The effective guide truly accepts the task of controlling the behavior of the person to whom he is giving guidance. There are times when he must seem to "play God," that is, to decide what is best for the person for whom he is responsible, or for his society. Parents in particular have the final responsibility for their children, and this responsibility cannot be put off on someone else.

Those of us who are teachers sometimes have the responsibility of failing a student in a course, dropping a graduate student, or failing to admit a student to college or graduate school. This is what teachers are paid to do—exercise their best judgment in such situations. To withhold the positive reward may be personally difficult, but it is necessary for several reasons. One of these is to maintain personal integrity, of course. A second is to provide accurate informational feedback to a person about the desirability of his responses. If he is told that a poor response is in fact satisfactory, he will then be selecting his future responses on the basis of false assumptions, engendered by the false feedback. Finally, the guide will not be perceived as trustworthy if he makes evaluations of responses on the basis of his own personal likes and dislikes.

Unfortunately, the guide often cannot just refuse to make any reaction. As has been pointed out before, the mere failure to act in some situations is in fact one course of action. The guide must consider himself to be the person best qualified to make the decision about the proper act, if a more qualified person is not available. If the guide fails to act, then the subject-person probably will learn undesired behaviors. To administer discipline to another person requires maturity and self-discipline. If the best judgment of the guide is that an act should be unrewarded or punished, it is his responsibility to do this. Often I have heard parents say that they cannot bring themselves to punish a child, even though they know they should. This behavior is selfish and represents indulgence on the part of the parent toward himself, rather than toward the child.

The guide must be willing to work for the goals he has established. To this end, he should develop within the person he hopes to guide a positive feeling toward the guide himself. This is necessary for the effectiveness of certain rewards, like verbal praise, smiles, and caresses. The principle to be employed is substitution learning, in which the guide himself is associated with pleasant states of affairs. Different personalities of guides will, to some extent, control the particular kinds of approaches they use to accomplish this association.

The guide should know when more or less guidance or control of the subject-person is needed. He should recognize that more guidance is needed early in the development of an act and that the guidance or control should decrease as the person develops more independence and skill in accomplishing the act.

The guide should recognize his own limitations. For example, he should understand that treatment of severe emotional problems requires specially trained professionals who have studied many years for the purpose. An insufficiently trained person will very likely aggravate, rather than cure, a serious emotional problem.

Summary

This chapter discusses the ways in which acts are acquired and lost. The key principle is that rewarded acts tend to be repeated, and non-rewarded acts tend to be replaced by different ones. Learning may not be evident at first, but it will be revealed when the person has the desire to perform the learned acts.

Different learning situations include trial and error, stimulus substitution, perceptual discrimination, and insight. Rewards are highly preferable over punishments to guide learning. Punishments tell the person what not to do, rather than what he should do.

The need for consistency in rewarding acts was pointed out. Although every desired act does not have to be rewarded every time it occurs, an undesired act should never be rewarded. The effectiveness of many rewards depends upon a personal positive regard for the guide by the person who is being guided.

The progression of learning was described in terms of an S-shaped curve; for totally new acts the progress is slow at first, accelerates to a rapid pace, and then decelerates until the act becomes very well learned. Perfection of performance is virtually impossible to achieve for very difficult tasks.

Several hints for promoting learning were offered: rewards should be large and frequent; the key to eliminating nonadjustive acts is to replace them with incompatible acts; very difficult acts should be established by shaping, or rewarding successively improving approximations to the desired act; overlearning, or learning beyond minimal level of mastery of an act, improves retention of the learned act.

11. A Benediction

The first purpose of this chapter is to commend the reader for reading this far. Because this is a practical book, you are obviously trying to increase your ability to work harmoniously with others. Those of you who are parents are particularly commended because you are trying to improve your guidance skills in order to take up the responsible role of guiding your child. Too many parents are voluntarily leaving this role to the school, the church, or some governmental agency. Similarly, I salute the youth who read this book for seriously preparing to take an adult role in society.

Goals and Responsibility

As discussed in chapter 9, the guide has the problem of helping the subject-person set goals. A main—but not the only—consideration in setting these goals is what the guided person wants for himself. As we have discussed, the guide is only then reassured that the subject person is working toward his own goals.

So that he is not misled into thinking that what is best for himself is also necessarily best for the person to be guided, the guide must first understand his own self. For example, parents typically want their children to have or to achieve more than they themselves have enjoyed. But some parents try to live substitute lives through the lives of their children. The high aims of such persons for their children are really aims of their own; the selected goals are not necessarily in the best interests of the children. In such a case, the parent is likely to put ultimately harmful pressure on the child to achieve the parent's goal.

The guide always has the problem of knowing how much freedom to give the person and what limits to set on his behavior. We ask the question, "Who is responsible when the person goes wrong?" One easy answer—but not necessarily the correct one—is that the general society has failed. This would be argued from a deterministic point of view. Similarly, one could easily blame the particular guide, using the same argument. Another tempting answer from the point of view of the believer in complete freedom of will is that the person himself is responsible for all of his failures. In my view, no one source is completely to blame, because none has complete control over all of the factors that enter into the molding of a person's behavior—not the general society, not the parent, not the person himself, certainly not his teachers. To the extent that each has had an input, however, he shares the responsibility.

Ultimately, we must hold each person responsible for his own acts when he is mature enough to make responsible choices, even though we know that others should share the blame. Once having said this, however, we still understand that the parent, the teacher, and society in general share responsibility for the misbehavior of society's members. The guide must have a strong enough conscience to feel sufficient guilt if he has failed. Without this sense of responsibility, he is not likely to work hard enough at his job.

Admittedly, too much guilt for failure to give effective guidance is also bad. If one has truly tried his best to give guidance, guilt will not be productive. It may in fact harm the mental health of the guide. Feeling guilt also may lead the guide to make maladaptive acts, as when a parent tries to reduce his feelings of guilt by giving his child things that the child ought not to have.

The final choice of the right acts is determined jointly by what is best for the individual person and for the society as a whole. The choice of specific acts involves judgments about values and as such is beyond the scope of this book. The guide must nevertheless decide which are the acts to reward. Once the desired goals are clearly in mind, then firm purpose is needed to work toward them. Many parents need someone to tell them that what they are doing is right and proper. I hope this book does that.

Value of Sincerity

The idea of shaping the behavior of another is easier to accept if one feels that he is doing it out of a sincere interest in the welfare of the other person. Leonard Doob (1948) points out that the propagandist who tries to control the behavior of others is not necessarily insincere. Doob says,

> Like the missionary, he may resort to tricking or employing subtly misleading devices to obtain converts, but God and his conscience approve (p. 278).

It is therefore important to understand our own desires in order to know whether we are doing something for the good of another or for our own personal good. How does one get to be sincere? The guarantee of sincerity is to work only for those goals of which you yourself approve.

The above point is relevant to the choice of specific techniques for the guidance of learning. The problem of the guidance technique is to establish the similarity of the learning situation to the future situation to which the learning is to be transferred. How do you train the subject inside the home or classroom for the environments which can occur outside the teaching situation? How do you teach a child the proper responses for, say, his first job application? Many of the conditions of the interview cannot be anticipated. The most effective avenue, in my opinion, is to develop (educate) a confident, secure person, by establishing a home atmosphere that is sincerely warm, loving, and supportive.

Be on the side of the person you are guiding. Have confidence in your ability to see faults, regardless of whose they are. Give obvious evidence of your concern for the other person by taking his side when he is right. In the case of a child in school, for example, it is important to support the school if you can, but, if the school is wrong, you must firmly support your child. I have found this to be necessary several times in raising my own children. Fortunately, as a psychologist, I felt confident enough in what I believed to make a protest. Unfortunately, I have known some cases in which the parents accepted a poor decision by the school system because they believed that the presumed experts were necessarily correct.

Memory Aids

The following simple aids to memory are given to the prospective guide by way of summary. The five main principles of the book are summarized by five "Cs": Conviction, Control, Consistency, Compassion, and Courage.

Conviction

Conviction concerns the setting of goals. The guide should be convinced that the goals selected for the subject-person are right and appropriate for him. Thus, the guide can have the conviction and confidence that he is working for the proper goals, that the established limits for acceptable behavior are fair and reasonable. He can therefore work toward those goals without continuously questioning whether he is doing the right thing.

Control

Control refers primarily to the shaping of behavior by the use of rewards. These should be used consciously and conscientiously to establish the proper behavior. The guide should not be reluctant to use the tools of behavior modification in order to be of help to the person he is guiding.

Consistency

The guide should reduce possible confusion by structuring the situation with consistent reward for behavior toward the selected goal. Never reward behavior which moves toward some conflicting goal. Inconsistency jams the machinery of the person, making it impossible for him to function effectively.

Compassion

The guide should have sympathy for the problems of a person trying to adjust to the complex society of today. Learning is usually a slow process, even when the learning situation is clear and unambiguous, which it usually is not in our society. People make mistakes. Also, if the guide has compassion, the subject person will probably understand this, and a beneficial climate for interaction between the two persons will be generated.

Courage

The guide needs the courage to continue the course that he has selected and believes to be right. Sometimes when he attempts to direct and shape the responses of another, that person resents it—at least consciously. Some persons cannot tolerate displeasure with them by others, and will thus be poor guides. There are times when the parent or boss must say no, even though this is unpopular with their subject-person, and also possibly with a few kibitzers from the sidelines.

The other necessary aspect of courage is to keep from becoming discouraged if great progress is not soon apparent. Depending upon where one has to start, the progression of learning may be very slow.

Words of Encouragement

The final goal of this chapter is to encourage the reader to use basic psychology. A guide must not become discouraged if the task before him seems impossible. The human being is marvelously adaptive and can survive many mistakes in handling. When the person turns out "bad," many mistakes have happened many times. The person can survive psychologically despite numerous mistakes by his guides; if this were not true, I suppose we would all be psychological cripples.

A child is continually testing the limits established by the parent. He is always pushing for more freedom. This is healthy. As he grows, he is given more freedom, and he is continually testing to learn when more will be allowed. This very process, as the child is growing up psychologically, is hard on the parent. As a parent, I found it discouraging to muster my psychological resources to get a ground rule established for the children one week, only to have it challenged again the next week—and the next. But one alternative to this—to crush the spirit of the child by making him fearful of, and dependent upon, authority—is not likely to produce an effectively functioning, problem-solving adult. Another alternative to this—to therefore abolish the rules—will probably also harm the developing child. The child develops his psychological "muscle" by straining against restrictions, just as physical muscles are strengthened by pushing against opposing forces. The muscle which is saved from harm in a protective cast becomes shrunken and progressively more useless. The personality that is similarly protected from wounds and strains will also wither.

Children are often able to take advantage of their parents' love for them. Parents are sometimes too close to the situation—too emotionally involved—to administer the correct guidance. Often the correct guidance requires punishment of the child or the withholding of something that the child strongly desires. Frequently, parents do things against their better judgment because the kids beg for it. Whenever I gave in and let my children do something against my better judgment, I was invariably sorry for it later when the results became apparent.

The main point of this discussion is to encourage the guide to do what he knows is right. The story is told about the farmer who asked the county agent what job the agent was supposed to do. The agent replied that his job was to show the farmer better ways to grow his crops. The farmer replied that he had no need of the county agent because he failed to do as well as he already knew how to do.

The guide has some factors in his favor. He is typically older, wiser, and more experienced, and he of necessity has some control over the person he is to guide. For example, parents have the power to control their children if they will exercise it while the child is young. If the parent is not blinded by his love for the child—if he is not ruled by emotion instead of reason—he should be able to outsmart the child easily. It must be remembered, however, that the child is working at it continuously; he does not have the responsibilities which prevent the adult from working full time at getting his own way. One of the reasons that we do not always do as good a job as we know how to do is that we frequently do not have complete control over the situation. As one of my colleagues said with respect to the rearing of children, "Just when you are ready to do the right thing, the telephone rings."

An old saying illustrates the value of training for discipline in the home. It says essentially that it is better to learn discipline in the home, where there is love, because otherwise it will be learned in the outside world, without love.

Progress in guidance will probably not proceed smoothly and consistently toward the desired outcome. The process of learning a new act always shows reversals or inversions. This means that some gains will be followed by some losses. The total progress of learning will, therefore, be irregular. One needs a perspective of the total view to see that there is a general trend of improvement. Often some learning is occurring even when there is no improvement in performance over many trials. This learning may result in a later spurt in performance, if the guide does not become discouraged and quit. Occasionally, too, the person will show insight, and jump straight to the proper performance with little or no additional training. As was pointed out in chapter 10, even this rapid learning depends upon a person who has the proper background, built up through varied experiences over many trials. But the guide should look for, and be gratified by, small gains as well.

Although positive results might not show up immediately, "sleeper" effects are possible. That is, the desired act may show up in behavior many years later as the person develops and matures. He might have developed the correct views, but the effects of the views may be revealed only later when the person matures and thus ceases to respond primarily on the basis of his desires, and becomes more influenced by his views.

As was brought out in chapter 7, it is impossible for any two people to have perfect interpersonal communication—of necessity, each person's internal world is private. Other people can understand an individual's world only imperfectly, through his verbal reports and through his actions and reactions in certain testing procedures which have been developed by psychologists. Therefore, there will always be communication gaps—between generations, races, ethnic groups, and nations, as well as between individuals. Although we should work to close the gaps as much as possible, we should not be distressed if this goal cannot be achieved completely.

Other people have problems, too, about which even persons close to them may be unaware. Even the generally secure person may have moments of fear or anxiety, without any objectively rational basis. For example, a friend of mine told me one day that his son had a dream that his father was going to kill him. The possibility of such a murder was ridiculously remote, of course. Assuming that our daytime fears cause our nocturnal dreams, we might, with some justification, infer that the boy had a twinge of concern when he was awake about some potentially hostile act of his father's. Therefore, we must understand that others too can have doubts about their ability to handle problems in their lives, even though they may appear on the outside to be perfectly in command and totally confident. Probably everyone needs encouragement from time to time.

Finally, and I think this is most important, a per
admit mistakes, for surely he will make some. Al
may seem discouraging, rather than encouragi
number of opportunities for making a mistake in i
is so great that it is probably impossible for anyon
record of correct responses. A few mistakes will
effort, particularly if the guide does not worry ab
them to himself and to others.

Glossary

Abnormal: not normal; the abnormal act can be less desirable than normal, or more desirable.

Achievement: the degree or level of success attained.

Act (or action): what a person or animal does; a unit of behavior; usually identified in terms of the purpose it achieves.

Adjustment: performing acts to solve problems; bringing the arousal to desired levels.

Aggression: attack on another person or group.

Analysis: separating the subject of study into its smaller parts for easier study.

Aptitude: the initial ability or potential to acquire proficiency with experience.

Assimilation: process of integrating one fact or situation into a group of facts or situations so that it becomes a tolerable or even harmonious part of the whole.

Behavior: anything an animal does, including gross voluntary acts, responses to external stimulation, muscular movement and glandular response, and other physiological activity.

Behaviorism: the view that psychology as a science studies only observable behavior; unobservable events are inferred from these observable behaviors.

Clairvoyance: supposed awareness of events which are not perceptible by any known sensory system; a more familiar term for E.S.P.

Classical: first in class or rank; standard.

Classical Conditioning: Pavlovian type of learning in which two stimuli are presented together until the unlearned response originally given to the one is now given as a learned response to the other; also referred to as respondent conditioning.

Code: a set of rules or laws for representing and associating information; a system of signals for translating information from one form to another; provides meaning to the input a person receives.

Cognition: general term for any process by which a person obtains knowledge of an object; includes perception, recognition, conception, judgment, and reasoning.

Compulsion: overpowering tendency to perform an inappropriate act which the person consciously tries to avoid.

Concept: a general notion or idea for several things which have similar characteristics.

Conditioning: learning; includes classical and instrumental situations.

Conscience: a person's evaluation of an act with respect to whether or not it has been in harmony with his consistently held views.

Correlation: method of science which examines what inputs and internal conditions are present when the person performs certain acts; an empirical relationship between two events.

Counterconditioning: elimination of undesired behavior by having the individual learn a different act in the presence of the original stimuli.

Data: the factual material used as a basis for discussions and conclusions about behavior.

Decision: choosing which act to perform.

Delusion: false belief, held in spite of sufficient evidence against it.

Depression: general sadness or lowness in "spirits" or mood.

Desensitization: process of decreasing emotional reaction to a stimulus by exposing the person to it under conditions not likely to produce the strong emotional response.

Desire: a want or wish for something.

Diagram: an explanatory line drawing to represent relationships between things.

Discrimination: responding differently to two different inputs.

Displacement: giving an act in the wrong situation, in response to an inappropriate stimulus.

Education: a kind of learning which is oriented toward the general improvement of the person to enable him to respond adjustively in many unspecified situations.

Emotion: a condition of feeling, such as fear, anger, grief, joy, which combines both psychological and physical arousal.

E.S.P.: see Extra-sensory perception.

Experiment: method of science in which some condition is changed and the person's acts are examined to see if they are thereby affected.

Extra-sensory perception (E.S.P.): supposed perception by means of some sensory system other than the known senses.

Fact: something known to be true, or to have actually happened; potentially verifiable by at least two competent observers.

Feedback: the sensory signalling of the result of a behavior; information about the outcome of a response.

Final common path: a group of nerves funnelling nerve impulses from the connective centers in the brain to the organs which produce the responses.

Fixation: performing the same act over and over again in a situation even though that act may not be adequate or effective.

Formal: according to regular or established form or custom.

Free will: idea that a person can by personal choice select the act that he will do.

Frequency: number of times something happened, or the number of persons doing some act.

Frustration: unpleasant feeling when a person is blocked from the achievement of what he desires.

Generalization: responding in the same way to two different inputs; acting as if the inputs were equivalent.

Graph: simple drawing to show how two things are related, such that an increase in one thing is associated with an increase or decrease in the other.

Guidance: process of helping another person select those acts which will produce for him effective adjustments and mental health.

Guide: person who helps another by giving guidance.

Habit: learned tendency to make a particular response in the presence of a particular stimulus.

Hallucination: a false perception of an object when no stimulus for it is present.

Hormone: chemical substance produced by an organ of the body which causes some physical or psychological effect.

Hypothesis: a possible explanation for a given act, which is not known to be true, but which is suspected to be true.

Illusion: a false perception of a stimulus so that it is perceived as being different from the way it actually is.

Incentive: an object or condition which a person perceives as being able to satisfy one of his desires.

Inhibition: restraining or stopping a process, or preventing it from starting.

Input: the stimulation of the person; the psychological environment (technical term: stimulus, singular; stimuli, plural).

Insight: sudden understanding of the solution to a problem on which one has been working; the parts of the solution are suddenly "put together."

Intelligence: capability of a person to learn and to solve problems quickly.

Intelligence Quotient (I.Q.): a measure of intelligence computed by dividing a so-called mental age by the person's chronological age (up to about sixteen years) and multiplying by 100 to remove the decimal (see Mental age).

Interaction: used in a general sense, this means that two or more systems exert a mutual influence on one another; in a more technical sense it refers to the phenomenon in which an effect of one factor is changed—either increased or decreased—when some other change in a situation is made; in this latter sense we can say that the effect on behavior of a given factor depends upon the total situation in which that effect is to be observed. A statistical description of this effect is called "interaction variance."

Introspection: looking inside oneself; reporting personal experiences such as feelings and sensations.

Learning: a relatively persistent change in an animal or human which is due to experience and which is inferred from a change in behavior.

Machine: a thing having more than one part, which is built to accomplish some work.

Maturity: high development in body and mind; ability to tolerate frustration; capability of delaying or denying satisfaction of desires.

Mean: the arithmetic average; it is obtained by adding the values for all cases and dividing by the number of cases; the term "mean" is preferred to the term "average" in the psychological literature.

Mechanism: a part of a machine which enables it to perform its function.

Mental Age: the score on a test achieved by the average child of a certain chronological age, up to about sixteen years.

Mental Health: the condition of feeling satisfied with life and enjoying it.

Mind: a conception of a total class of permanent structures that control behavior.

Mood: temporary state of mind or feelings.

Motivation: the process by which certain desires produce certain acts.

N: the total number of cases, instances, observations, subjects, etc.

Negative: denial; characterized by resistance or reverse reaction to suggestion or stimulus; counterproductive; opposite of positive.

Normal: the strength of act that is close to the center of the normal distribution; the degree of closeness to the center is not specified absolutely; usually assumes that the distribution was obtained from an unselected (normal) population of persons.

Objectivity: freedom from personal bias; degree to which judgments are unaffected by personal desires.

Obsession: overpowering tendency to pay attention to, or to be haunted by, thoughts which the person would rather not think about.

Operant: behavior in which the individual operates on the environment in some way to produce an effect; the specific stimulus to which the individual is responding might not be identified; when used to identify a type of learning, it refers to the instrumental or trial-and-error approach.

Overlearning: learning which has progressed beyond the degree necessary for reaching a minimally acceptable criterion.

Perception: reception and interpretation ("making sense") of the input.

Personality: the sum of a person's psychological characteristics which determine his behavior.

Philosophy: a consistent conception or system of principles about the universe, the aim of which is to understand reality.

Phobia: persistent excessive fear that is without a reasonable basis.

Positive: affirmative and constructive; productive; opposite of negative.

Principle: a fundamental truth for guidance.

Process (noun): active way of treatment by which a change in a person or thing is produced.

Process (verb): subjecting a person or thing to an active treatment which will change him or it.

Profession: the work that a person does to earn a living.

Psychokinesis: supposed ability of a person to influence by mental effort the movement of inanimate objects, such as the rolling of dice or the turning of cards; the supposed "mind over matter" effect.

Psychology: the study of the causes of acts; the study of behavior.

Psychosomatic: refers to the relationship between psychological functioning and body structures.

Psychotherapist: person with appropriate training who tries to help another solve his psychological problems; the training may be obtained in any of several ways, for example, psychologists are usually trained in graduate schools of psychology, whereas psychiatrists are physicians who take residencies in the medical specialty of psychiatry; psychoanalysts are psychiatrists who are trained in the tradition of Sigmund Freud.

Punishment: stimulus that produces dissatisfaction, pain, or denial of satisfaction; it is not desired by the person.

Quack: untrained person who is not qualified to do what he claims.

Rationalization: construction of a false reason to attempt to justify an act.

Reasoning: putting together two habits which were not previously connected, in order to solve a problem.

Reflex: inborn connection between a certain stimulus and response.

Regression: returning to an earlier and less mature act, after a more mature level of behavior has already been reached.

Reliability: dependability; the degree to which a measuring instrument or process can be counted on to give similar results if the measurement is repeated.

Respondent: behavior which is given in response to a specific stimulus; the Pavlovian or classical type of learning.

Response: the unit of behavior, voluntary or involuntary, which may be small, e.g., a muscle twitch, or large, e.g., an integrated purposeful act.

Reward: stimulus that produces satisfaction in the person because it is desired (technical term: positive reinforcement).

Rote: repetition in a mechanical, routine way, without attention to meaning; requires no understanding but merely exact reproduction of stimuli in their original form.

Scapegoat: a person or group unjustifiably blamed for frustrations and disappointments; recipient of displaced aggression.

Science: a group of facts about nature and the process of searching for such facts.

Self-esteem: image or view the person has about himself; it may be favorable or unfavorable, high or low.

Set: readiness to take a given view, or perform a given act; can be very transient, like a momentary focusing of attention, or very stable, like a basic attitude of a person.

Shaping: changing behavior to be more like the desired acts by applying the proper rewards for successive improvements.

Sleeper effect: a change in behavior which was not present earlier but which appears later; a latent effect of learning, for example, which may at first imply that no learning has occurred.

Species: a distinct kind of animal or plant, in which all members of the group have the same permanent characteristics.

Standardization: establishment of exact procedures for giving a test and for identifying the group of persons on which the test results are based.

Statistics: quantitative procedures to show the numerical relations between facts.

Stereotype: a fixed, oversimplified concept of something.

Stimulus: object or event which influences acts by activation of a sense organ; actually it is not the object or event itself but its representation (excitation in the receptor organs) which is the true stimulus.

Stimulus bound: condition in which the behavior of the person is essentially controlled by the stimulus input.

Stress: extreme psychological arousal produced by an excess in intensity or complexity of inputs, thus putting excessive strain on the adjustive mechanisms of the person.

Subject: person or animal whose actions are manipulated, observed or otherwise studied.

Telepathy: the supposed communication between one mind and another by means other than the known senses and physical methods of communication.

Therapy: treatment intended to promote mental health.

Training: the kind of learning which is oriented toward the development of skills to accomplish a known job in which the necessary responses to be learned can be anticipated.

Transfer: carry-over of learned performance from one stimulus situation to another.

Trauma: any physical or psychological injury to the person.

Unconscious: those views, decisions, or desires of the person which are unknown to him.

Validity: foundation in truth, fact, or law; the degree to which a measuring or testing process measures correctly what it is supposed to measure and purports to measure.

View: a way of looking at something, which determines the perception and cognition of it.

Bibliography

American Psychological Association. *Ethical Standards of Psychologists.* Washington, D.C.: American Psychological Association, Inc., 1953.

American Psychological Association. *Ethical Principles in the Conduct of Research with Human Participants.* Washington, D.C.: American Psychological Association, Inc., 1973.

American Psychological Association. "Revised Ethical Standards of Psychologists." *A. P. A. Monitor* 8 (1977):22–23.

Bindra, D. *Motivation: A Systematic Reinterpretation.* New York: Ronald, 1959.

Brady, J. V. "Ulcers in 'Executive' Monkeys." *Scientific American* 199 (1958):95–100.

Bruner, J. S. *The Process of Education.* Cambridge, Mass.: Harvard University Press, 1960.

Bruner, J. S., and Minturn, A. L. "Perceptual Identification and Perceptual Organization." *Journal of General Psychology* 53 (1955):21–28.

Carmichael, L.; Hogan, H. P.; and Walter, A. A. "An Experimental Study of the Effects of Language on the Reproduction of Visually Perceived Form." *Journal of Experimental Psychology* 15 (1932):73–76.

Dewey, J. *Problems of Men.* New York: Philosophical Library, 1946.

Dollard, J., and Miller, N. E. *Personality and Psychotherapy.* New York: McGraw-Hill, 1950.

Doob, L. W. *Public Opinion and Propaganda.* New York: Holt, 1948.

English, H. B., and English, A. C. *A Comprehensive Dictionary of Psychological and Psychoanalytic Terms.* New York: Longmans, Green and Co., 1958.

Freud, S. *A General Introduction to Psychoanalysis.* Garden City, N.Y.: Garden City Publishing, 1943.

Gagné, R. M. and Fleishman, E. A. *Psychology and Human Performance.* New York: Holt, 1959.

Guthrie, E. R. "Conditioning: A Theory of Learning in Terms of Stimulus, Response, and Association." In *The 41st Yearbook of the National Society for the Study of Education, Part II,* edited by N. B. Henry. Chicago: University of Chicago Press, 1942.

Harcum, E. R. "Effect of Prerecognition Exposures on Tachistoscopic Word Perception." *Perceptual and Motor Skills* 19(1964):855–860.

Hebb, D. O. *The Organization of Behavior.* New York: Wiley, 1949.

Mandler, G. "Emotion." In *New Directions in Psychology,* edited by E. Galanter, R. Brown, E. H. Hess, and G. Mandler, pp. 265-343. New York: Holt, Rinehart, and Winston, 1962.

Menninger, K. *The Vital Balance: The Life Process in Mental Health and Illness.* New York: Viking, 1963.

Orbison, W. D. "Shape as a Function of the Vector Field." *American Journal of Psychology* 52(1939):31–45.

Pavlov, I. P. *Conditioned Reflexes.* Translated by G. V. Anrep. London: Oxford University Press, 1927.

Raspberry, W. "Testing Minorities." *Newsweek,* September 23, 1974, p. 19.

Roethlisberger, F. J., and Dickson, W. J. *Management and the Worker.* Cambridge, Mass.: Harvard University Press, 1939.

Rosenthal, R. *Experimenter Effects in Behavioral Research.* New York: Appleton-Century-Crofts, 1966.

Silberman, C. E. *Crisis in the Classroom.* New York: Random House, 1970.

Skinner, B. F. "Superstition in the Pigeon." *Journal of Experimental Psychology* 38(1948):168–172.

West, L. J.; Pierce, C. M.; and Thomas, W. D. "Lysergic Acid Diethylamide: Its Effects on a Male Asiatic Elephant." *Science* 138(1962): 1100-1102.

Wyatt, D. F., and Campbell, D. T. "On the Liability of Stereotype or Hypothesis." *Journal of Abnormal and Social Psychology* 46(1951):496–500.

Index